THE
ECONOMICS
OF JUST ABOUT

EVERYTHING

ANDREW LEIGH

THE ECONOMICS
OF JUST ABOUT

EVERYTHING

ALLEN&UNWIN
SYDNEY·MELBOURNE·AUCKLAND·LONDON

We gratefully acknowledge the Estate of W. H. Auden for permission to reproduce an extract from 'As I walked out one evening' from *Another Time* by W. H. Auden, published by Random House. Copyright © 1940 W. H. Auden

We gratefully acknowledge Tim Minchin for permission to reproduce lyrics from his song 'If I didn't have you'. Copyright © 2008 Tim Minchin

First published in 2014

Allen & Unwin
83 Alexander Street
Crows Nest NSW 2065
Australia
Phone: (61 2) 8425 0100
Email: info@allenandunwin.com
Web: www.allenandunwin.com

Cataloguing-in-Publication details are available
from the National Library of Australia
www.trove.nla.gov.au

ISBN 978 1 74331 471 5

Index by Puddingburn
Cover and internal design by Alissa Dinallo
Set in 11.5/18 pt Minion Pro by Midland Typesetters, Australia
Printed and bound in Australia by Griffin Press

10 9 8 7 6 5 4 3 2 1

CONTENTS

Introduction

How do bad incentives delay babies and kill convicts, what's a
rule of thumb you can use when shopping for clothes, and why
is economics like a blue guitar?

On the evening of Wednesday, 30 June 2004, 33-year-old Cathy
Swales of Sunbury, north of Melbourne, sat very still at home
and sipped a cup of tea. Already 39½ weeks pregnant, she waited
gingerly for the hours to tick by.[1]

Swales had good reason to be nervous. The previous month,
Treasurer Peter Costello had handed down his ninth budget,
proudly announcing that the parents of all babies born on or after
1 July 2004 would receive $3000 from the government.

Because the policy came into effect just two months after the
announcement, it could not affect when people became pregnant.
But could such an incentive lead those who were already pregnant
to delay births? Asked by a reporter 'Would it have been better to
have announced and introduced this policy at the same time?',
the health minister stammered, 'Well if I thought that mothers

1

would put their babies at risk, but I don't believe mothers would put them at risk.'[2]

At the heart of the issue was a fundamental economic question: how much do people respond to incentives? To test this, Joshua Gans and I teamed up to crunch the numbers.[3] Our approach took the same form as many of the studies you'll read about in this book: get as much data as possible, from as many sources as possible, then look for patterns.

In this case, it would have been hard to miss the result. For the previous three decades, the number of babies born each day in Australia had hovered at around 600. On 30 June 2004, it spiked downwards. Then, on 1 July, Australia recorded 1005 births which was then the highest number of babies born in a single day since records began. The 'baby bump' continued well into mid-July. Altogether, we estimated that more than 1000 births were moved from June 2004 to July 2004.

How did parents manage to shift births? The answer lies in the fact that around half of all births are medically induced or delivered by caesarean section. Indeed, when we broke down the data by birth procedure, we saw that the number of caesarean sections and inductions was significantly higher in July than June. Conversely, vaginal births (without an induction procedure) stayed constant. Parents were responding to incentives.

Amused by our results, we decided to see whether incentives might matter at the other end of life.[4] Just as incentives affect when a person is born, could they affect the timing of death?

We cast our eyes back 25 years earlier, to 1 July 1979: the day on which federal inheritance taxes were abolished. For those leaving estates over $1 million, inheritance taxes were 28 per cent.

As in our births study, we compared the last week of June with the first week of July. And again, we found a significant difference. We estimated that around 50 fewer people died in the final week that the Australian inheritance tax was in operation. On the face of it, this might seem to be a smaller impact than the Baby Bonus, but that could be because inheritance taxes only affected about one in ten of those who died in 1979. Once we take this into account, it looked to us as though about half of those who would have paid inheritance taxes if they had died in June 1979 managed to shift their date of death to July 1979. Now that's what I call dying to avoid taxes.

How do people shift their date of death? One possibility is that families were considering whether to turn off life support. Another is that through force of will, people were able to hang on for another week. It's also possible that descendants misreported the date of death to the authorities. Unlike the Baby Bonus study, we can't be sure precisely how so many people managed to avoid inheritance taxes in the final week: we just know that they did it.

One of the core principles of economics is that people respond to incentives. In the words of Chicago University's Gary Becker, a pioneer of the 'economics is everywhere' movement, economics comes down to 'maximizing behaviour, market equilibrium and stable preferences, used relentlessly and unflinchingly'.[5] In the case of the Baby Bonus, you could see the health minister flinching as she considered the incentives that her government's policy had created.

If there are two themes to this book, they are that economics is everywhere, and economics is fun. If your eyes glaze over when you read the business pages of the newspaper, don't worry. This is not a book about the terms of trade and deflation—important as those topics are. In these pages, you'll see how the ideas of economics can illuminate questions as diverse as sport and dating, dieting and art. Some of these topics don't have anything to do with money. The study of economics has been described as legitimating self-interest, a 'greed is good' philosophy. But in fact, economics envisages people maximising wellbeing and happiness, not financial rewards. Economics can explain the behaviour of both Scrooge McDuck and the Dalai Lama.

Over recent decades, there has been a revolution in economics as our discipline has broadened its scope. Top young academics are working on everything from child soldiers to racial profiling, newspaper bias to the effects of television. After assessing a batch of newly minted academics from elite universities, Princeton economist Angus Deaton observed: 'Twenty years ago, there was essentially none of this.'[6]

And yet the *Freakonomics* revolution has taken too long to get to Australian universities. With a handful of exceptions, antipodean economists tend to focus on more traditional topics. Over the coming years, I hope we will see the economics of everything shaping the way in which we teach economics at the high school and undergraduate level. Perhaps it might help to boost enrolments in economics, currently the discipline of choice for just one in 50 Australian undergraduates.

Let's take a simple example of how economics can help you solve everyday problems. Suppose you're at the beach and decide to treat yourself to a soft-serve chocolate-dipped ice-cream. It's a scorchingly hot day, and just as you go to take a bite of the ice-cream, it slips out of your sweaty hand and falls into the sand. Seeing this, the seller calls out, 'Would you like to buy another?'

At this point, many of us would angrily kick the sand and walk off. But economics tells us that if you have enough cash in your hand, the right answer is almost certainly yes. The first ice-cream is gone, so you should ignore it when making your decision. If you were willing to pay the cost of an ice-cream one minute ago, you should be willing to do so again now. In economic jargon, you should make your decision *at the margin*.

Applying economic thinking can literally mean the difference between life and death. In 1790, the Second Fleet set sail from England. Unlike the First Fleet, which was organised by the British Government, the Second Fleet was a commercial operation. The three main ships of the Second Fleet, *Surprize*, *Neptune* and *Scarborough*, were contracted from shipping firm Camden, Calvert & King, which had previously been involved in the trans-Atlantic slave trade. The firm were paid a flat fee of 6 pennies for each convict who departed. Accordingly, they packed nearly 1000 convicts onto the ships.

The five-month voyage was one of the most brutal in shipping history. To keep costs down, the crew was recruited from local taverns. They were brutal to the convicts, with floggings routinely administered. Convicts received starvation rations, apparently so that some of their food could be sold upon arrival. Prisoners were kept below deck and in leg-irons. Scurvy ran rampant. By the time the ships docked in Sydney harbour, the convicts were covered in lice. Around one-third of those who had left England were dead, and many of the survivors could barely move or speak.[7]

When news reached England, there was an outcry. But Camden, Calvert & King had already begun preparing the Third Fleet of convicts, which would set sail in 1791. So the government changed the payment mechanism, stating that contractors would be paid on results, with around 20 per cent of the payment depending on the convict arriving in good health.[8] On this voyage, there was less overcrowding and considerably better treatment of the convicts. The death rate was one in eleven.

The improvement between the Second Fleet and Third Fleet shows the different trade-offs that the shipping company chose to make. When paid by the number of convicts that departed the shores of England, the firm opted for more convicts and a higher death rate. Once they had a financial incentive to get convicts to Australia alive, they chose a different trade-off: fewer convicts per ship, more rations per convict and better treatment on board.

Remember Gary Becker's comment about 'stable preferences'? In the case of people who ship convicted criminals around the world, this means assuming that if they cared more about making money than saving convict lives in 1790, they would probably hold the same attitudes in 1791. So if you want to stop ships' captains killing convicts, your best starting point is that the captains' views are stable.

The idea of stable preferences is particularly important when we're dealing with ugly views. I find the behaviour of the captains and crews of the Second Fleet repugnant. I don't think attempts to change their views (say, by putting the Third Fleet through a series of ethics seminars before setting sail) would have been as effective as changing the incentives.

Economists are fond of finding similar patterns across time and place. We have been known to apply our toolkit to studying pirates and drug addiction, polygamy and witchcraft. Indeed, economists have played games with capuchin monkeys, a tropical South American primate.[9] The monkeys were offered the chance to exchange tokens for different types of food, such as apples versus grapes. Experimenters varied the number of tokens required for each type of food (the price) and the total number of tokens each monkey had at its disposal (their wealth). The results follow expected patterns, with capuchin monkeys buying less of different types of foods as they became more expensive.

Economists aim to make a complex and uncertain world a little more comprehensible. We start with theories—about incentives, preferences, marginal thinking and so on—and apply them to data. Economists tend to use larger data sets than most other social scientists. When I did my PhD in the early-2000s, I analysed a survey with over a million respondents, and researchers today work with data sets that are much larger than that. Economists also worry a great deal about identifying causal patterns. Just because roosters crow before the sun comes up, it doesn't follow that roosters cause the sun to rise. If you want clever tricks to separate correlation from causation, economics is the discipline for you.

In this book, I'll introduce you to some of the economic findings of my own academic research, carried out during the six years that I worked as an economist at the Australian National University. I'll also roll my sleeves up and look at new data, producing some fresh results that may surprise you. One of the great joys of economics is to ask a question to which we don't know the answer—and there's plenty of that in here.

In the coming pages, you'll meet the ideas of economics in a variety of different disguises. In Chapter 1, I'll see what economics has to say about love. Is there really a marriage market? And what can economics teach you about speed dating? In Chapter 2, I look at what the field known as 'behavioural economics' has to say about living a healthier life. If you're trying to quit smoking, lose weight or sleep more, economics might have some answers.

Moving from fit to super fit, Chapter 3 studies sport, and how economics can be used to determine the all-time best batsmen and the most productive AFL team—as well as the role of luck in shaping careers. Chapter 4 looks at wages, and how your gender, height, education and beauty affect your pay packet.

Chapter 5 analyses career cycles, seeing what we can learn about career success from studying Australia's great painters, musicians and novelists. In Chapter 6, I'll look at a different kind of career—the world of crime. It turns out that incentives can shift behaviour, even on something as dramatic as committing a murder. Chapter 7 turns the economic spotlight onto global poverty. I discuss the scarcity problems faced by people living on less than a dollar a day, and explore how the ideas of comparative advantage apply to foreign aid.

In Chapter 8, I study the economics of forecasting. How good are our crystal balls when it comes to predicting recessions, exchange rates and the jobs of the future? Can economics help to predict a great wine vintage—even before it's been bottled? Finally, Chapter 9 draws the strands together, with a few concluding thoughts on how economics can help you make better decisions, and maybe even live a more interesting life.

The great Oxford philosopher Isaiah Berlin once divided thinkers into hedgehogs, who know one big thing, and foxes, who know many little things. This book is an amalgam of the two approaches (which I guess makes me either a hedgeox or a foxhog). It aims to convey a few big ideas about economics, but to do so through a plethora of facts and stories.

A common myth among non-economists is that economists care only about money. If you believe the legend, we're the people who would sell our grandmother to the highest bidder and then bribe the judge to get off. In my experience, top economists—particularly those in academia—care *less* than most people about money.[10]

So why do people think economists are obsessed with money? Perhaps one reason is that we often convert things into dollar terms to make a comparison. For example, a friend of mine once told me about her rule of thumb when buying a new item of clothing: spend no more than $2 per wear. If a pair of shoes looked like she would wear them 50 times, she would pay up to $100 for them. But if a skirt looked like she would only wear it ten times, she would only let herself pay $20 for it. Exceptions could be made for fancy-dress costumes and wedding dresses.

This kind of thinking is known as cost–benefit analysis: sum the costs, sum the benefits, and compare the two. It's a simple way of making decisions at an individual, business or government level. Yet it's surprising to see how often people want to give the impression of carrying out such analysis without actually putting it into action. For example, in my day job, I'll often meet with lobbyists who have commissioned 'economic research' to draw attention to their cause. Actually, all they've done is taken the cost of a problem—such as cancer, dementia or bullying—and put a dollar figure on it.

Unlike cost–benefit analysis, 'cost analysis' doesn't help us decide what to do. The point of putting a price on a malady is to compare it with the benefit of a remedy. Adding up costs alone is a bit like saying that a ski trip will leave you poorer and sorer. It's probably true—but not the whole picture.

Thanks to behavioural economics, we also know that there are systematic ways in which we deviate from the rational model. At a certain point, more options don't make us better off. In one experiment, a tasting booth showing 24 jam flavours drew more customer attention, but one with six varieties sold more jam. Three-year-olds who are allowed to choose from among a hundred different toys are less happy than children who are told to play with a single toy. Companies have sometimes increased sales by reducing their product range.[11]

We also tend to be lemming-like in our preference for the status quo. (Actually, that's unkind to lemmings, since we now know that the myth came from Disney documentary filmmakers in 1958 who deliberately flung lemmings over cliffs.[12]) Still, the metaphor of blindly following the person in front does sum up how we make many daily decisions. We are more likely to eat the dish at the top of the menu than the one at the bottom. Our mobile ringtone is probably the default factory setting. Our superannuation is most likely invested in the default fund, with the default investment plan.

Behavioural economics reflects the fact that choosing can be hard. We don't have the time of a monk or the skills of an actuary. In fact, the representative citizen is closer to Homer Simpson than to HAL, the supercomputer from *2001: A Space Odyssey*. Humans have a surprisingly strong bias towards immediate gratification but there are simple strategies to combat this tendency. If you tend to put off studying for exams, then choose courses that involve continuous assessment. If you find yourself making credit card purchases that you later regret, why not delay impulse purchases by storing your card in a glass of ice in the freezer?[13]

The insights from behavioural economics require us to create richer models of the world, but they don't debunk standard economics. For most of the problems you'll face in your life— ranging from 'Should I get a tattoo?' to 'Should I ask my boss for a pay rise?'—it makes sense to think in terms of trade-offs and incentives, to do cost–benefit analysis and ignore sunk costs. Non-economists all too often pretend that resources aren't scarce, and that people's preferences will change. They ignore comparative advantage, and they don't think on the margin.

The economic approach is not the only reasonable way of viewing the world, but I hope that by the end of this book you'll come to recognise the power of economic thinking. In his poem 'The Man with the Blue Guitar', Wallace Stevens tells the story of a guitarist who was asked why he did not play things 'as they are'. The musician responded that things as they are 'Are changed upon the blue guitar'. Economics is my blue guitar. I hope you like the songs.

For love or money

How should an economist date online, can you find true love with imperfect information, what are your odds of divorce and what is the surprising geography of same-sex couples?

Located in far north Queensland, 400 kilometres inland, the town of Mount Isa sits atop vast deposits of lead, silver, copper and zinc. Mining is a male-dominated industry, so the town has had more men than women for about as long as anyone can recall. In 2008, then mayor John Moloney decided to take action to rectify the gender imbalance, announcing: 'if there are five blokes to every girl, we should find out where there are beauty-disadvantaged women and ask them to proceed to Mount Isa'.

Asked by a journalist whether he thought such women would have a better chance of finding a partner in Mount Isa, Moloney replied, 'I would think so. It would naturally seem that there may well be less competition.' Local Anna Warrick, a 27-year-old single occupational therapist quickly hit back, responding, 'We've got a saying up here that the odds are good, but the goods are odd.'[1]

What is striking about the Mount Isa example is that the town's gender ratio was only mildly skewed (in the 2011 Census, the town had 11,325 men and 9,912 women, nowhere near the mayor's five to one ratio). And yet even a small tilt had both the mayor and Mount Isa's single women feeling that the odds had shifted. One of the core ideas in economics is 'market equilibrium'. If we regard dating as a market, then a monogamous equilibrium requires a similar number of men and women. Mount Isa was in a different equilibrium—one in which more men than women were single. Put another way, there was 'male unemployment' in the Mount Isa dating market.[2]

In the case of Mount Isa, it took a gender imbalance to get people thinking like economists about the dating market. By the end of this chapter, I hope you'll recognise that 'the economics of everything' even has something to say about matchmaking.

The economc perspective on marriage is perhaps best summed up by Tim Minchin's song 'If I Didn't Have You'. The song begins:

> *If I didn't have you to hold me tight*
> *If I didn't have you to lie with at night*
> *If I didn't have you to share my sighs*
> *And to kiss me and dry my tears when I cry*
> *Well I really think that I would . . .*
> *Have somebody else*
> © Tim Minchin 'If I didn't have you'

After surveying the other possible people he might have gone on to love, Minchin decides:

> *It's just mathematically unlikely that at a university in Perth*
> *I happened to stumble on the one girl on Earth specifically*
> *designed for me*
>
> © Tim Minchin 'If I didn't have you'

The bewildering array of possible romantic options confronting young people brings to mind The Whitlams, who noted that if the object of their desire was one in a million, then 'there's five more, just in New South Wales'.

So what's a desperate and dateless economist to do?[3] The economics of dating comes down to three simple rules:

1. There is no perfect match, but some matches are definitely better than others.
2. You won't know how well suited you are to someone until you get to know them.
3. Time is scarce, so a decision based on limited information is probably better than no decision at all.

The challenge in dating is that you don't have enough information, and you don't have enough time to get it. To give you an idea of just how severe the problem is, let's imagine that you're aged 18 to 25, and you're trying to find the person you're best suited to in that age range.

To begin, there are about 1.5 million men and 1.5 million women to choose from. If you picked a sex, and spent only three minutes with each of those people, then it would take 25 years of speed dating to find the person you liked the most. Things are harder still if you want more than three minutes to assess each person, if you're bisexual, if you want someone older or if you think true love resides overseas.

Fortunately, economic theories are rarely deterred by problems involving large numbers. Better yet, economists are familiar with precisely this kind of problem. It's called an 'optimal-stopping problem'.

The idea of an optimal-stopping problem is simple: you must choose a time to stop in order to get the best outcome. You can choose when to stop. Information is produced by a random process, and each day you get some new information. If you never stop, you get an outcome that isn't particularly attractive, so, at some point, you probably want to stop.

In 1875, Cambridge University mathematician Arthur Cayley came up with the first optimal-stopping problem, which looked at gambling games.[4] Since then, the approach has been applied to a raft of other life questions. If you're trying to sell your house, at what point should you accept an offer that's lower than your asking price? If you're looking for a job, which job should you settle for? If your car is having mechanical problems, when should you trade it in? If you're fishing, when should you call it a day?

But the most interesting application of optimal-stopping problems is romance. Like most other optimal-stopping problems, no one is forcing you to stop searching for the right person to love. Similarly, you could never sell your house, always stay unemployed, keep your car until it stops in the middle of the freeway or do nothing but keep fishing. For most people, a life of dating is in the same category.

How should you carry out your search? One insight is that just as when buying a house, you should gather as much information as possible. My unscientific poll of economists suggests that most like the idea of speed dating and online dating, since these search techniques offer the potential to garner more information about potential matches.

Because online dating generates large data sets, and economists enjoy analysing large data sets, the two are a natural fit. In general, the research throws up few surprises: men and women have a preference for people who are of similar age, income and education, and of the same race.[5] Among heterosexual couples, women have a stronger preference for high income, while men have a stronger preference for good looks.

Things get more interesting when economists study the behaviour of people who use online dating. About four-fifths of the time, it is men who make the initial contact. Of 100 emails sent by men to women, fewer than four end up in a first date.[6] While some couples agree to meet after just a few emails, it takes on average six emails to get to a first date. Online daters are surprisingly choosy.

Online dating is already changing relationships, with one study finding that a fifth of those who use dating site RSVP ended up getting married as a result.[7] The internet is also making it possible for people to get together who might never have met otherwise. On a flight to the United States a few years ago, I sat next to a Brisbane woman who had worked as a retail assistant. She had met her boyfriend, a helicopter pilot from Houston, on eHarmony. He had earlier flown out to spend a week with her in Australia, and she was now moving to Texas to live with him. A computer algorithm had brought them together.

Internet dating is particularly important for people who are looking for something different. For a young gay man in a small country town, online dating provides a way of meeting potential partners that's probably safer than the offline alternatives. The same goes for people who are looking for a partner of an unusual race, ethnicity, religion or body size. This helps explain Australian sites such as Two of a Kind (for Jewish couples), Aussie Men (for gay couples) and Mature Match Maker (for older couples).

Online dating isn't without its risks, since anyone can pretend to be someone they aren't (as a famous *New Yorker* cartoon put it: 'On the Internet, nobody knows you're a dog'). Anyone using online dating is advised to follow basic rules such as googling the person they are chatting with, not sending money to a person they haven't met and arranging the first meeting in a public place. But the technology does offer the potential to help join up couples who might never have found one another without the web.

Other studies have analysed speed-dating events, in which groups of men and women meet in a structured setting, and take it in turns to have short conversations. After the conversation, each person records whether they would like to exchange contact details (this is called a 'proposal'). If both say yes, the organiser provides them with each other's contact details.

One research team analysed the data from a British speed-dating company, whose events attracted an average of 22 men and 22 women.[8] The typical male participant made five proposals, while the typical female participant made three proposals. Because women were more selective, one-third of male participants ended the night with no matches, as compared to just one-tenth of female participants. On average, taller men, slimmer women and non-smokers received more proposals. Having children did not affect the number of proposals (though it's quite possible the topic didn't arise in most three-minute conversations).

In another study, US economists set up their own speed-dating program, using students at Columbia University in New York. This allowed them to collect data on intelligence (university entrance scores) and attractiveness (based on having independent raters assess photographs of the speed daters). Not surprisingly, they found that women placed more importance on intelligence, while men placed more importance on beauty. More curiously, they observed that women had a strong preference for partners of their own race, while men did not. (Other studies have found strong racial preferences among both men and women.)[9]

Because the US research team were running the speed-dating sessions themselves (rather than crunching data afterwards), they were able to see what happened as they increased the number of participants. When the sessions had ten men and ten women, both men and women proposed to half of those present. When the number of participants was doubled to twenty men and twenty women, men still proposed to half the women, while women became more selective, proposing to around one-third of the men. They explained the finding by quoting a *New Yorker* cartoon that depicts a group of men and women at opposite ends of a bar. The thought bubble above the men reads 'Select All', while the one above the women reads 'Select None'.

While online dating and speed dating can tell you a bit more about your romantic options, there's only so much you can learn from emails and a three-minute conversation. To solve the optimal-stopping problem that is modern love, you'll have to get to know your potential match a little better.

Here's where things get tricky. In some optimal-stopping problems, information comes along in an instant. For example, if you're selling a house, you know immediately whether a bid is larger or smaller than the one before it. If you're fishing, you know the size of each fish as you pull it over the edge of the boat. In other optimal-stopping problems, it's not immediately obvious whether you've found a great match. If you're job-hunting, you won't really know whether a firm is a good fit until you've worked there for a while. And if you're looking for love, then as Tim Minchin has noted, love is not 'destined perfection' but an 'affection' that 'grows over time'.

So here's the problem when you meet someone: you need to work out whether you like them and they need to work out whether they like you. Then, the longer you spend together, the stronger a bond you'll form.

Sounds tough, doesn't it? But the economics of relationships isn't too dismal. In fact, theory and empirical evidence suggests that love matches may be on the rise. It's a result that comes from my friends Betsey Stevenson and Justin Wolfers of the University of Michigan—an economics couple who collaborate on research on a variety of topics, including the economics of the family. Stevenson and Wolfers pointed out that a century ago, the norm was for fathers to be the breadwinner, and mothers to be the home-maker.[10] Because both partners specialised, the incentive was to look for someone based on their ability to do something you couldn't do. That meant young men were looking for a great home-maker, while young women were looking for a great breadwinner.

Today, things have changed considerably. Although remnants of traditional gender roles still persist, most mothers these days do some paid work, and most fathers help out around the home. More than ever before, both parents are a combination of bread-winner and home-maker. So today's twenty-somethings are less likely than their grandparents to be looking for someone who has *different* skills and abilities. Instead, they're more likely to be looking for someone who can do *similar* things to them. More than ever before, young people have the freedom to look for a soul mate.

Indeed, the evidence seems to suggest that as incomes rise, people are more likely to be in love. Gallup survey data for 113 nations asked people whether they experienced love during the previous day. In the poorest nations, about six in ten people say yes. In the richest countries, the share rises to seven out of ten.[11] While some respondents could have in mind non-romantic affection (e.g. to a parent or child), it's possible that the Beatles were wrong: money can buy you love.

If love works out well, you might even decide to tie the knot. Whether or not to marry is a personal question, but the economics are straightforward. Imagine a young couple, Kim and Chris. They would like to enjoy a monogamous relationship together but each knows that they might be tempted to cheat. Marriage helps raise the social cost of cheating by giving it a new name ('adultery'), and making it a breach of a promise they've made in front of their friends. From Kim's perspective, marriage may help prevent Chris from straying (if he is, in Hillary Clinton's famous words, 'a hard dog to keep on the porch'). But even if Kim is the one most likely to cheat, she may favour marriage because it helps prevent her from putting short-term temptation ahead of long-term happiness.

Forgoing short-term happiness for long-term gain is a notion grounded well before the birth of economics. In Homer's epic poem *The Odyssey*, Odysseus wanted to hear the Sirens, beautiful sea creatures whose enchanting song lured sailors onto the rocks. He solved it by having his sailors put beeswax in their ears, and then tie him to the mast. Whatever he said when the Sirens started singing, he told them, they were not to untie him: 'Firm to the mast with chains thyself be bound / Nor trust thy virtue to the enchanting sound'.[12] Like Odysseus tying himself to the mast, the marriage contract can sometimes make us happier overall by helping us avoid temptation. (In the next chapter, we'll look at similar issues in the context of health economics.)

If you opt to get married, you'll probably participate in a ritual that has its roots in economics: the purchase by the groom of a valuable engagement ring for the bride. Engagement rings have their origins in an era when potential husbands placed great value on a bride being 'pure'. Once engaged, couples might—shock! horror!—spend time alone together. This meant that if a man called off the engagement, his fiancée might not be able to find such an eligible match in the future. She was therefore to keep the engagement ring as compensation. Despite major shifts in social norms about pre-marital sex, the tradition of expensive engagement rings continues to this day.

Yet no matter how expensive the ring, some marriages will end in divorce. Just as the internet helps couples find their first love, it probably acts as a technological spur to infidelity (indeed, the United States now has a website called Ashley Madison, devoted entirely to those seeking extramarital affairs). Perhaps contrary to the stereotype, women initiate divorce nearly twice as often as men.[13]

The average divorce probability masks considerable differences across the community.[14] Using a data set of nearly 7000 people,

I crunched the statistics on divorce according to three things: how old you were when you got married, whether you finished high school, and how long you've been married. The results are shown in Table 1. In the first decade of marriage, the highest divorce rate is among those who didn't finish Year 12 and were married as teenagers. Of these couples, 23 per cent will split up in the next five years. By contrast, for those who finished Year 12 and married in their forties, the divorce rate is just 5 per cent.

A similar pattern persists among couples who have been married for more than a decade. The chance of splitting up is about twice as large for those who married as teenagers than for those who married in their thirties. In economic terms, you're less likely to find the best solution to your optimal-stopping problem if you stop (i.e., get married) when you're in your teens. Theory and data suggest that it's worth waiting until at least your twenties.

Table 1: Chance of divorce or separation in the next five years

	Age when married			
	Teenager	20s	30s	40s
Married less than 10 years				
Didn't finish Year 12	23%	11%	11%	10%
Finished Year 12	5%	9%	9%	5%
Married more than 10 years				
Didn't finish Year 12	5%	3%	3%	2%
Finished Year 12	7%	4%	2%	4%

Note: Average rate of divorce or separation over a five-year period: 5%

Perhaps surprisingly, whether a couple has children doesn't seem to affect their probability of getting divorced. But, as you delve more closely into the data about divorce, a curious pattern emerges. Among two-child families, those with a boy and a girl seem to have different marriage rates than those with two boys or two girls.

To understand why this might be so, let's go back to the notion of preferences. Standard economics suggests that if there are two things that I might enjoy, then my ideal is probably to have a mix of the two rather than just one. That's because the more you have of something, the less you tend to enjoy each additional unit. It's great to have one bicycle, but the second bicycle probably doesn't bring as much happiness as the first. It's great to have a fortnight's holiday, but another fortnight probably won't be as much fun as the first fortnight. In economic jargon, the *marginal* enjoyment that people get from something diminishes the more they have of it. So the average person is more likely to choose one bicycle and a fortnight's holiday rather than two bicycles and no holiday (or no bicycles and a month's holiday).

This brings us back to children. Sons are amazing. Daughters are amazing. But as any parent can attest, boys and girls are different. Whether because of nature or nurture, boys are more likely to be found kicking a football, while girls are more likely to enjoy ballet. So it's not unreasonable to think that the typical couple might prefer a boy and a girl to having two girls or two boys.

I set out to answer this question using Australian Census data.[15] My starting point was the fact that parents with two boys or two girls are more likely to have a third child than those with one boy and one girl. This gave me the clue that parents with two children of the same sex might be a little less satisfied. Analysing the data for over 20,000 couples, I found strong evidence in favour of the theory. Among two-child families, parents with two children of the same sex are nearly 2 per cent less likely to be married than those with a boy and a girl. Unfortunately, unlike the marriage results, these findings turn out to be practically useless. All of us get to choose when to get married, but none of us get to choose the gender of our children.[16]

Still, those of us fortunate enough to be able to have children usually get to choose how many to have. And here, economics can offer some insights. Children increase your expenditure. A middle-income family will spend about $800,000 to raise two children from birth until they finish their education.[17] This includes $160,000 on transport, $140,000 on food, and $100,000 on recreation.

In thinking about the cost of children, a non-economist might stop there. But if you want a full estimate of the costs, it's not enough just to measure expenditure—you also have to look at forgone income. If having children causes you to miss out on a dollar of earnings, that's an economic cost as much as if they cause you to spend another dollar. Put another way, economics teaches us that you don't have to pay for something for it to be an economic cost.

In the case of children, taking account of the full economic cost makes a big difference. On average, women with children take a career-break after the birth, and are more likely to work part-time while the children are young. This not only lowers their immediate earnings, but also reduces their labour market experience, which means they earn less in the future. The lifetime cost of this for the typical mother with two children is $600,000.[18] Add that to the expenses ($800,000) and the cost of two children for the typical Australian family is $1.4 million.

So how many children should you have? Economics doesn't give a single answer, but it does urge you to think about how your decision will affect your happiness over a whole lifetime. As you juggle nappies and sleep deprivation, you might wish you didn't have any. As a happy grandparent, you'll wish you'd had a dozen. For most of us, the right answer is probably somewhere in between. The optimal answer isn't just what's right for now—it's what's right, on average, over your life.

Until now, I've focused on heterosexual couples, but that's not the full picture. According to the 2011 census, 0.7 per cent of Australian couples are same-sex couples. Of these, about half are gay couples and half are lesbian couples.[19] The share of same-sex couples reported in the Census has more than doubled since 1996. This probably reflects both an actual increase in same-sex couples, and a greater willingness to report sexuality honestly in the Census. Social norms on same-sex relationships are changing fast, as reflected in the removal of explicit discrimination from dozens of statutes and the powerful push for same-sex marriage.

Surveying the data brings some surprises, and confirms some stereotypes. Gay men are most likely to work as retail managers, while women in same-sex couples are most likely to work as nurses. People in same-sex couples had higher household incomes and better education levels, were less likely to be religious, and were more likely to share the housework. About half of all heterosexual couples have children, compared with about one-fifth of lesbian couples, and one-thirtieth of gay couples.

According to one economics study, we can even use the distribution of same-sex couples across Australia to tell us something about city quality. The approach aims to solve an old problem in urban economics: working out which places are the most liveable. The problem arises because other indicators tend to be unreliable. House prices capture not only whether a city is a nice place to live, but also the quality of local jobs. Expert rankings depend on how you weight factors such as weather, congestion and restaurant quality.

So—the argument goes—why not look at where same-sex couples choose to live? Since they have more disposable income, surely we'd expect to see same-sex couples gravitating to the most liveable places? Using this approach, economists Dan Black, Gary Gates, Seth Saunders and Lowell Taylor concluded that the three most liveable cities in the United States were San Francisco, Washington, DC, and Austin, Texas. Applying the approach to Australia, it appears that the most liveable cities are Sydney and Canberra (both with 1.1 per cent same-sex couples), with the bronze medal going to Melbourne (with 0.9 per cent same-sex couples).[20]

In one *Seinfeld* episode, Jerry hires an attractive maid to clean his apartment, and then begins dating her.[21] When his new girlfriend stops bothering to clean the apartment (but keeps taking Jerry's money), a horrified Kramer tells Jerry that he is now effectively paying for sex. Jerry eventually tells the woman that the relationship is over—and that she's fired. Love and money can be a hazardous mix.

The same goes for romance and economics. If you're convinced that economics has something to teach us about love, marriage and the family, then I need to tell you one more secret. There may be 50 ways to leave your lover, but there's only one way to use these economic insights into romance, and that's tactfully. You may be solving an optimal-stopping problem, but divulging this insight on your first date may mean that it's also your last.

Similarly, if you're a man who's about to go down on bended knee, I do *not* advise you to describe the engagement ring to your fiancée as compensation for the fact that her value on the marriage market is about to fall. Blokes in the maternity ward: please *don't* blurt out 'Darling, did you know that second boy statistically lowers our odds of staying together?' to a woman who's just experienced excruciating pain delivering your child.

Love may mean never having to say you're sorry. But if you start talking about loveonomics to your partner, you may find yourself saying sorry quite a bit. One option is to slowly start talking economics at the dinner table, and hope that the pennies drop. An even easier strategy is just to buy another copy of this book for your significant other. That way, they can work out for themselves that the main reason you married them was to increase the cost of infidelity for both of you.

2

Fit for tomorrow

Would you pay yourself to quit smoking, why have SUVs become so popular, is obesity a problem of diet or exercise and how does an economist get to bed on time?

At his heaviest, comedian Mikey Robbins weighed 150 kilograms. For a long time, he said: 'I knew . . . I didn't look good'. One of the hardest parts of the day was shaving 'because it was the one time of the day where you actually had to look at yourself in the mirror. Basically I was like this big jowl of skin that started at the cheekbones and just sort of hung down there'.[1]

Other things were hard too. His liver function was abnormal, and he was borderline diabetic. He snored so loudly his wife had to sleep in another room. Being heavy made life complicated. When he saw a flight of stairs, Robbins had to think about where the lift was. Before sitting down, he had to assess whether the chair would take his weight.

A friend described Robbins as having 'an addictive personality'. His wife, Laura Williams, was amazed by how much he could eat. 'He would just graze the whole day. He'd be lying on the couch with a bowl of pistachios, or some cheese, he just did not stop eating.'

Robbins, in his battle with his weight, represented an internal challenge that many of us face. Do we have that chocolate dessert now, even though we know we'll regret it tomorrow? Will we go for a lunch-time walk on a cold winter's day or stay inside where it's warm?

Today, some of the biggest health conundrums we face—both as individuals and as a society—are what economics calls 'time-inconsistency problems'. From smoking to speeding, overeating to under-sleeping, we're too often tempted to make decisions that make us happy today at the expense of tomorrow.

Analysing the way we make decisions over time has been a major focus of the field known as 'behavioural economics', which you can think of as the love child of economics and psychology. While its precise date of birth is disputed, behavioural economics came to prominence in the 1990s. Like most love children, there was a bit of embarrassment about it at first but the vast majority of economists now accept behavioural economics as part of the discipline. When you hear commentators talking about economics as a field that doesn't understand psychology, they're describing the way the discipline was in the 1980s—not how it is today.

A key insight of behavioural economics is that we seem to treat time in inconsistent ways. Standard economics recognises that we might 'discount' the future. Faced with a choice between a 15-minute massage today versus a 20-minute massage tomorrow, many would opt for the former.[2] But what's hard to reconcile with standard theories is that when faced with the choice of a 15-minute massage in seven days versus a 20-minute massage in eight days, most will choose the latter. In both cases, the choice is the same: a one-day delay gets a massage that's five minutes longer. But when it's today versus tomorrow, we behave differently from the way we behave when the choice is between something in seven days' time versus eight days' time.

Similar thinking affects what we eat. A clever experiment on self-control invited participants to choose between free fruit or free junk food, to be collected in a week's time.[3] Half chose fruit, and half chose junk food. When they returned a week later, all participants were given the option of changing their choice. Now, five out of six chose junk food. As the joke goes, what's the easiest day of the week to start a diet? Tomorrow.

Behavioural economics has implications for many fields of economics, but none more than health. In this chapter, I'll discuss four of the major health challenges facing Australia: smoking, road safety, obesity and sleep. Improvements in these areas could make us a healthier nation. Economics helps us to understand why progress in all these areas is hard.

Let's start with smoking. One of the most poignant emails I've received from a constituent read as follows: 'My great-grandfather, grandfather, father and one of my uncles all died from smoking-related conditions. Each of the latter three died 20–30 years before the life expectancy for their generation. My father's addiction contributed to two decades of poor health prior to his premature death, resulting in frequent periods where he was unable to work.'

History's first smokers were Native Americans, who burned dry herbs in wooden pipes. After Christopher Columbus' voyage, Spanish explorers brought tobacco back to Europe in the 1500s. But smoking only became commonplace after American James Bonsack invented a machine in the 1880s that would mass-produce cigarettes. Cigarette prices fell, and by 1945, three-quarters of Australian men and one-quarter of Australian women were regular smokers.[4]

There's no mystery as to why people smoke: it's pleasurable. I've never had a cigarette, so let me quote from an expert on the topic. Here's Richard Klein, professor of French literature and author of *Cigarettes are Sublime*:

Take a long, deep puff on a cigarette, fill yourself up with its venomous smoke; let it touch the innermost convolutions of your lungs; then exhale it, slowly, past nose and lips in a swirling, expanding stream about your head. Tout est là . . . Joining inside and out, each puff is like total immersion: it baptises the celebrant with the little flash of a renewed sensation, an instantaneous, fleeting body image of the unified Moi.[5]

Cigarettes are also deadly. They are the only legal product that—if consumed as directed—will kill half their users. They are extremely addictive. Ask smokers if they plan to quit, and 92 per cent say yes.[6] So the economics of smoking is a time-inconsistency problem: how do we help people say no to a pleasurable activity now in order to save themselves from a heart attack, lung cancer or gangrene in the future?

The answer is a mix of incentives and information. Over the past generation, the cost of a cigarette (in today's dollars) has risen from 40 cents to 70 cents. Because young people are particularly price-responsive, this has significantly reduced the take-up rate among schoolchildren. Studies show that on average, a 10 per cent increase in cigarette prices reduces smoking rates by 5 per cent.[7] The other incentive is cheap nicotine patches. Since 2011, patches that previously cost $4 a day have been available at $1 a day to anyone with a doctor's prescription.

Australia has also run major public awareness campaigns about the risks of smoking, and has banned cigarette advertising on radio, newspapers and television for more than two decades. In 2012, Australia became the first nation to require that cigarettes be sold in olive-coloured boxes without logos, a move prompted by studies showing that adolescents were less excited by cigarettes in plain packages.[8]

It's not just adolescents who are affected by information campaigns. Looking to explain why Europeans smoke more than Americans, one economic study found that Europeans were less likely to believe that smoking harms your health. Indeed, even when the study authors restricted the analysis to non-smokers, they found the same pattern: for example, while 94 per cent of American non-smokers think smoking is harmful, only 84 per cent of German non-smokers share the same view. Like the United States, Australia has been successful in spreading the message that smoking kills.[9]

Today, Australian smoking rates are 18 per cent for men and 14 per cent for women—about half what they were in 1980.[10] From an economic standpoint, this has occurred partly because of information campaigns, which emphasise to people that they are making a trade-off between pleasure now and pain later. There has also been a shift in incentives: raising the cost of buying cigarettes, and lowering the cost of quitting. Incentives can even help in other ways. For example, one study in the Philippines offered smokers the chance to put their cigarette money into a savings account for six months, after which they took a urine test for nicotine.[11] If they tested negative, they got the money back. If positive, they lost it. One-third of those who signed the contract successfully quit smoking.

Yale University economist Dean Karlan, who co-authored the study, has since set up a website called stickK, which invites users to solve the time-inconsistency problem by making a contract with their future selves. An independent referee then assesses whether they have succeeded in quitting smoking by the given date. The incentive can be either avoiding shame (the system can notify your friends whether you succeed or fail) or getting your money back (you can put up as much or as little as you wish).

When a participant fails, the money will go to either a regular charity or an anti-charity (for example, a left-winger might pledge money to go to the George Bush Presidential Library). So far, stickK claims responsibility for more than 2 million fewer cigarettes smoked.

Another time-inconsistency problem is road safety. In January 2011, a car carrying six teenagers sped along Raymond Terrace Road, East Maitland, in the Hunter Valley in New South Wales.[12] With an inexperienced driver at the wheel, it spun out of control on a bend and crashed into a row of trees. Seventeen-year-old Alana Boyd and fourteen-year-old Stephanie Drain were killed. Boyd's injuries were so bad that she could only be identified by a tattoo. The two girls were among 1277 Australians killed on our roads that year.

For joy-riding teenagers, road deaths are often a consequence of putting pleasure now ahead of being alive tomorrow. Driving at 150 kilometres per hour without a licence might be a thrill, but it's hard to imagine that it's in anyone's long-term interest to give it a shot. For others, road accidents are simply a consequence of trying to save time. The typical Sydneysider now spends 340 hours a year—the equivalent of fourteen full days—commuting to work.[13] It's little wonder that they're tempted to squeeze through a red light or drive a few clicks over the speed limit.

As for smoking, our society has managed to find ways of helping people solve the time inconsistency problem of driving dangerously. Seatbelts have been mandatory across Australia since 1972. Australian police began random breath-testing in 1976, and started using radar speed cameras in 1985. From the late 1990s, states began reducing the speed limit on residential streets from 60 to 50 kilometres per hour. Speeding fines have risen, in many cases doubling in a decade. Cars have also become safer, with airbags evolving from a luxury in the 1980s to being commonplace today.[14]

Economists have shown that people change their behaviour in response to safety changes. For example, a famous study demonstrated that US drivers drove less safely when seatbelts became compulsory (a phenomenon known as the 'Peltzman effect'). Law changes in one area can also have health effects in others—as an economic study demonstrated by showing that compulsory helmet laws for motorcyclists reduced the supply of live organ transplants.[15]

Economists love nothing more than finding an unexpected effect of a law change. But even taking them into account, tougher traffic laws and better cars have clearly saved lives. Only about one-third as many Australians now die on the road as in 1970. That's despite the fact that there are more people, and a lot more cars. In 1970, there was one fatality for every 1250 cars on the road. Today, there is less than one for every 10,000 cars.[16]

But while the road toll is diminishing, there are still challenges. One is the rapid shift towards large four-wheel drives, increasingly known as sports utility vehicles, or SUVs. In 1980, SUVs made up one in 50 new car purchases—now they account for one in three new cars.[17] This is a massive change in the complexion of our new car fleet, and there's a simple economic explanation.

To see the economics of SUVs, we need to look at the accident statistics.[18] If you crash your large SUV, there's a 2.7 per cent chance you'll be killed or hospitalised. If you're driving a medium-sized car, those odds rise to 3.6 per cent. SUVs have better *crashworthiness* ratings, or in other words, driving an SUV makes you a smidgin safer.

The trouble is, things look different from the outside of an SUV. If you're in a crash with a large SUV, there's a 5.1 per cent chance you'll end up in hospital or the morgue. If you're in a crash with a medium-sized car, your chances are just 3.0 per cent. They may have better crashworthiness ratings, but SUVs score higher for *aggression* towards other road users (vehicles, cyclists and pedestrians). So if you're in a crash, an SUV makes you 0.9 per cent less likely to be killed or hospitalised, but makes everyone else 2.1 per cent more likely to end up under a white sheet. For every serious injury or death that is saved by switching from a medium car to a large SUV, two more result.

This is what economists call an externality—an effect you have on others that you don't pay for. Externalities can be negative or positive, but in the case of SUV drivers, they're clearly negative. Our publicly funded health-care system spreads the costs of hospital care across taxpayers, while in several states, no-fault or part-no-fault insurance spreads the cost of compensation across all drivers. Michelle White, an economist at the University of

California, San Diego, who has studied this phenomenon, has dubbed the rising size of US cars 'the arms race on American roads'.[19]

Now, back to time-inconsistency problems, with perhaps the biggest of them all: body weight. While smoking and traffic deaths are falling, Australian girths are widening. The most common metric used to assess whether you're overweight is Body Mass Index or BMI, which is your weight in kilograms divided by the square of your height in metres. Devised by Belgian scientist Adolphe Quetelet, the index is used to classify people into underweight (BMI below 18.5), normal weight (BMI 18.5 to 25), overweight (BMI 25 to 30), and obese (BMI over 30). Before he slimmed down, Mikey Robbins had a BMI over 40 (sometimes referred to as 'morbidly obese').

As any personal trainer will tell you, BMI isn't a perfect measure. Because it treats fat and muscle the same, BMI would have rated Arnold Schwarzenegger in his body-building heyday as 'obese'. But BMI does allow us to compare trends over time. In 1980, just over one-third of Australians were overweight or obese. Today, it's nearly two-thirds. Somewhere in the 1990s, Australia went beyond the point where it was normal to be in the 'normal' BMI range. Now, overweight is the new normal. In the latest analysis, 2 per cent of Australians were underweight, 35 per cent were normal weight, 35 per cent were overweight, and 28 per cent were obese. In 30 years, the proportion of Australians who are obese has more than tripled. Adjusting for age, the weight of the average Australian has risen by about one kilogram each decade.[20] A typical 40-year-old today is about three kilograms heavier than a typical 40-year-old would have been in 1984.

Why are we getting fatter? While there isn't a definitive Australian study, the economic research from the United States—which has seen a similar increase in waistlines—shows two distinct patterns. From the end of World War II until about 1970, the number of kilojoules that a typical person burned during the day declined. Fewer people walked or cycled to work. Desk jobs proliferated, and the percentage of people working in agriculture or manufacturing declined. That explanation holds until 1970, after which time the amount of energy we burn in a day has stayed pretty constant.[21]

Since 1970, the big change is that we've begun eating more. Nutritionists recommend eating a healthy diet that matches your energy need, which is typically about 9000 kilojoules a day for women and 11,000 kilojoules a day for men (although a person's actual energy requirement will vary with age, height and activity level). Food diaries show that the actual amount of food we consume is slowly creeping up. Every ten years, our average daily energy input goes up by another 300 kilojoules.[22] Each decade, we add the equivalent of another daily skim cappuccino to our diets.

The growth in girths over the past generation isn't primarily because we're doing less exercise, it's because we're consuming more kilojoules (and, in particular, more carbohydrates).[23] In economic language, the explanation has to do with inputs, not outputs.

The reason for this is that kilojoules are tastier, cheaper and available more quickly than ever before. Over the past few decades, a dazzling array of food technologies has helped to reduce the time between when we want a snack and when we can eat it. For example, modified atmosphere packaging takes a food packet and replaces the oxygen with carbon dioxide or nitrogen.[24] The effect is to dramatically reduce oxidation and the growth of bacteria. Other food technologies include stretch-wrap films, advances in artificial flavouring and the widespread availability of microwave ovens. The result is that cream-filled cakes—once the product only of ambitious cooks—can now be bought for only a few dollars. Tasty biscuits can be kept fresh enough to sell through a vending machine.

The consequence of these changes has been to increase how much we eat, and change when we eat it. According to US food diary evidence, while the amount of kilojoules consumed at dinner has fallen, breakfasts and lunches have more kilojoules, and the amount of energy consumed through snacks has nearly doubled.[25] Vending machines are extremely convenient, but also tempt us to do things now that we might regret later. If the vending machine is 10 metres away, a person on a diet might have a mid-afternoon snack. The same person is much less likely to have the snack if it requires a 10-minute walk to the corner shop.

Across the developed world, countries that have restricted the availability of new food technologies tend to have lower levels of obesity. But it is unlikely that Australia would want to turn the clock back on microwaves, vending machines and tastier foods.

This means the challenge is largely a personal one. According to a recent survey, more than half of all Australians are trying to lose weight.[26] While exercise matters, the simple fact is that successful weight reduction is more likely to be achieved by reducing inputs than increasing outputs (for example, a Snickers bar takes a few minutes to eat, but at least an hour's walking to burn off). So what dieting tips does economics have to offer?[27]

At the outset, it's useful to look at some lessons from behavioural economics about how we consume food. In a series of experiments, researchers have shown that a bigger plate, bowl or even pantry increases how much we eat. These results are consistent with the notion that we eat more with our eyes than our stomachs. We also eat more if we're distracted. In general, we consume less if we've already eaten in the past few hours, but when watching television, people end up eating just as much whether their stomachs are full or empty. In an experiment that combined both these insights, researchers gave containers of fourteen-day-old popcorn to movie-goers in Philadelphia. As they munched in front of the silver screen, those given large containers ate 38 percent more of the stale popcorn than people given medium-sized containers.[28] Similarly, people who say they stop eating based on external cues (for example, 'when my plate is empty') rather than internal cues (for example, 'when I'm full') are more likely to be overweight.

Applying these principles, a team of economists conducted an experiment that randomly assigned participants from a weight-loss website to one of ten weight-loss strategies. The two most successful dieting principles matched up with what behavioural economics would have led us to predict. The strategy of eating off a smaller plate (one with a diameter of 25 centimetres or less) saw participants lose an average of 0.9 kilograms in a month. Not eating while watching television led to a weight loss of 0.7 kilograms. Eating fruit before snacking led to a monthly loss of 0.5 kilograms. At the other end of the spectrum, the strategies of 'brushing your teeth when you feel like a snack' and 'eating oatmeal for breakfast' failed to keep the kilograms off.[29]

The final economic insight on dieting is to remember that being slim is not the only thing that counts. The more time you spend thinking about food, the less time you have to think about everything else (in defending why she gave up dieting, writer Natalie Kusz explained that she could not afford to give 70 per cent of her brain over to thinking about careful food choices).[30] A body-builder friend of mine who slimmed down for competitions by consuming protein shakes, lean meat and virtually no carbohydrates told me, 'I lost weight fast, but I couldn't concentrate on anything.' Advocates of complex diets often forget that time is scarce, and time spent monitoring every morsel means less time doing other things. To the economist, everything is a trade-off. A simple diet is probably easier to stick to.

Our final time-inconsistency problem is sleep. According to time use surveys, the typical Australian gets about 8 hours of sleep. But one-fifth of us kip for less than 6½ hours per night.[31] In some occupations, it's almost as though exhaustion is in the job description. A young lawyer working on a major case once billed the client for 270 hours in a single month, nearly twice as many hours as she would have clocked up if she had worked from 9 a.m. to 5 p.m. with a break for lunch. Her partner reportedly brought clean clothes to the office every few days, and she averaged just a few hours' sleep each night.[32]

The standard economic perspective on sleep is that higher wages make sleep less attractive.[33] The more you earn by putting in another hour on the job, the likelier you are to go to bed late and rise early. This helps explain why the rich sleep less than the poor, as well as why average hours of sleep have fallen over the past century. Moreover, the fact that wages rise over a person's life cycle may also account for the fact that 25-year-olds get more sleep than 45-year-olds (young children may play a role too). Indeed, sleep is negatively associated with the business cycle, suggesting that more red eyes on Martin Place and Collins Street may point to a strong economy.

There is clear medical evidence that too little sleep can be unhealthy. Physiologically, sleep allows the body to repair tissues and replenish hormones. Sleep deprivation has been linked to an array of health problems, including heart disease, diabetes and weight gain. In one experiment, patients were given a vaccine, and then kept awake that night.[34] A month later, their immune response was half that of patients who had a full night's sleep after getting the vaccine. Under-sleeping may allow you to live longer days, but perhaps at the expense of enjoying fewer years.

To test the effect of sleep deprivation on workers' productivity, an intriguing new strand of research takes volunteers into the laboratory and keeps them awake for 30–40 hours (the equivalent of pulling an all-nighter). They are then asked to complete tests alongside other subjects who are properly rested. In one experiment, sleep-deprived individuals were less willing to trust others. Another experiment indicated that sleep-deprived people did only about half as well on cognitive tests as their rested counterparts. Corroborating this, evidence from brain scans of sleepy and well-rested participants indicates that sleep deprivation leads to less rational and more emotional behaviour. In a road safety inquiry, one truck driver told the story of how long hours would sometimes cause him to hallucinate: 'I would see trees turning into machinery . . . On one occasion I held up the highway in Grafton while waiting for a truck not there to do a three-point turn (I was radioed by drivers behind me asking why I had stopped)'.[35]

In practical terms, employees who are untrusting, dim and over-emotional are likely to be bad for the firm's bottom line. Much of business is about knowing whom to trust and carefully balancing decisions on their merits. Without enough sleep, you may miss key details and make vital decisions based on gut instinct rather than careful reasoning.

Within the firm, sleep-deprived bosses who lose their temper are likely to cause subordinates to quit or slack off. On the road, sleepy drivers have the reaction time of drunk drivers, and contribute to at least a fifth of road deaths.[36] Perhaps it is no surprise that major accidents such as Chernobyl, the Challenger disaster and the Exxon Valdez oil spill are associated with sleep deprivation. And in a team that works at the pace of its slowest member, sleepy workers can cause decision-making processes to lag.

Getting more sleep is in your interests, and those of your employer. But, like the other time-inconsistency problems discussed in this chapter, there's a natural temptation to put pleasure now ahead of comfort tomorrow. At 11 p.m., I know that another hour of trash television will have me yawning into my espresso the next afternoon—but sometimes I just can't resist putting an excessively high value on today compared with tomorrow.

Among the strategies that 'sleep experts' propose are having a bed-time routine, avoiding caffeine in the evenings, and not drinking too much alcohol. On top of this, I find that I need to *raise the costs* of staying up late—such as by visualising the last time exhaustion made it painful to get through the next day. It also helps to *reduce the benefits* of staying up late—for example, by turning off my laptop and smart phone. That way, my cost–benefit calculation is more likely to come out in favour of shuffling off to bed.

Health matters. A famous economics paper set out to determine which has had the larger influence on society's wellbeing over recent decades: gains in life expectancy or gains in income. The researchers concluded that over some periods, life expectancy gains might have mattered more than increased income. Try the thought experiment yourself: since 1970, Australian life expectancy at birth has risen from 72 to 82, while Australian per-person incomes have risen from nearly $30,000 to nearly $60,000 (in today's dollars).[37]

If you could only have one of these extraordinary developments, which would you pick? Would you prefer to go back to an Australia where we only lived until 72, or an Australia where the average person only had $30,000? I've asked this question of lots of people, and I'm yet to find anyone—economist or non-economist—who'd sacrifice a decade of life in order to double their income in the remaining years. You'd end up with more income over your lifetime, but less happiness. For example, the fall in cancer death rates over the past quarter-century has saved around 7000 lives per year.[38] I'd rather have that outcome than be a smidgin richer.

Health economics reminds us that economics is about more than money. Increasingly, our health depends on the choices we make in our lives, and many of those decisions are what behavioural economists call time-inconsistency problems. How do we forgo the pleasure of a cigarette now for the greater lung function that a quitter enjoys? How do we avoid the temptation to drive a little faster than we should? Can we resist a delicious morning muffin? What makes it so hard to go to bed at a reasonable hour?

Solving time-inconsistency problems is a challenge in all our lives, mine included. I don't smoke but in my youth I drove too fast and these days I often stay up too late. Only the good fortune of genetics allows me to keep going through life as a fat man in a skinny body. I struggle with the same behavioural economics problem as most people: resisting the urge to do today what we know we will regret tomorrow.

Starting lineup

Who are the best Australian batsmen and the most efficient AFL teams, why are soccer players more likely to be born in August, and what happened to all those State of Origin fights?

Not long after retiring from test cricket, batsman Ricky Ponting walked out onto a local cricket pitch in the Launceston suburb of Mowbray. Ponting had captained the Australian cricket team, and scored more runs in one-day international and test cricket than any other Australian. Yet here he was, just months after retiring, back playing a game for the Mowbray Cricket Club, with hundreds of fans lining the ground for an autograph or photo, or to see Ponting in action.

By returning for a game of club cricket, Ponting reminded everyone that he was a true cricket tragic. At age eight, he would sneak into the Mowbray Cricket Club changing room and try on the players' cricket gear while they were out on the field. When he was given a baggy green cap at his test match debut, aged twenty, Ponting immediately put it to his face to see how it smelt. One cricket writer said of him, 'Ricky loves everything about the game. He loves the bats, the gloves, the shoes, the stories, the culture. He just can't get enough of it'.[1]

Malcolm Knox described Ponting as 'an aggressor who loves to confront bowlers; superbly balanced, he has a strong array of shots to every part of the ground'. Gideon Haigh said: 'He was vibrant, aggressive—perhaps even a little bit too aggressive at times. He was a kind of a touchstone in the Australian team. He was synonymous with success'.[2]

Ponting was good. But was he—as Michael Clarke has argued— 'the second best batsman Australia has ever had after Don Bradman'? To test this, we need to define success. In his analysis of great cricket batsmen, Griffith University economist Nicholas Rohde argued that success depends on two factors: batting average and career runs. Rohde pointed out that if the average was all that mattered, then the all-time best batsman would be West Indian Andy Ganteaume, whose average of 112 comfortably exceeds Don Bradman's 99.94. A good index, however, should take account of the fact that Ganteaume only scored 112 runs in his career, while Bradman scored 6996. Cleverly, Rohde weighted the two criteria by comparing batsmen to 'benchmark' players of their era.[3]

The following table shows Rohde's 'economic ranking' of best cricketers, based on results from test cricket matches from 1870 to 2013. On this analysis, Ponting comes in as the ninth-best batsman of all time, and the third-best Australian batsman, after

Allan Border. A crude ranking based on averages would have Ponting much further down the list (below English batsmen Ken Barrington and Wally Hammond, for example). Ponting's career contribution elevates him into the top ten, though the drop in his average in the last two years of his career saw him drop from seventh to ninth.

Table 2: An economic ranking of best cricket batsmen (1870–2013)

Ranking	Player (country)	Total runs	Average
1	Don Bradman (Australia)	6,996	99.94
2	Sachin Tendulkar (India)	15,921	53.78
3	Jacques Kallis (South Africa)*	13,140	55.44
4	Brian Lara (West Indies)	11,953	52.88
5	Garfield Sobers (West Indies)	8,032	57.78
6	Allan Border (Australia)	11,174	50.56
7	Rahul Dravid (India)	13,288	52.31
8	Sunil Gavaskar (India)	10,122	51.12
9	Ricky Ponting (Australia)	13,378	51.85
10	Steve Waugh (Australia)	10,927	51.06

* As at 24 November 2013.

Novelist Harry Crews once said that 'sports are just about as close to what one would call the truth as it is possible to get in this world'.[4] In the same spirit, the economics of sports is another way of getting towards economic truth. The Rohde ranking system recognises that each batsman picked for a team has an 'opportunity cost', which is equal to the value of the last man not chosen. Like a business that must choose between investing in one market or another, the economics of cricket recognises that the benefit each player adds to a team must be weighed against the value the next-best player would add.

Over recent decades, the economics of sport has come off the bench and onto centre-field for one simple reason: because researchers have shown that the sporting field can provide fundamental insights into human behaviour. In this chapter, I'll consider how luck can decide who gets on the field and who becomes a champion. I'll look at how crowd size and money affect the outcome of games. I'll consider the notion of 'competitive balance' and look at which are the most competitive Australian sports. But first, let's answer the question: where did the fights go?

In the 54th minute of the second game of the 2013 Rugby League State of Origin series, a fight broke out.[5] Annoyed at Paul Gallen's slowness to get off Jonathan Thurston, Queenslander Brent Tate pushed him away. New South Wales player Trent Merrin punched Tate, Queenslander Justin Hodges hit Merrin from behind, and New South Welshman Greg Bird joined in. What was surprising about the event wasn't that a fight broke out, but that it was relatively mild. Of the four players sent off, two claimed not to have thrown a punch.

For League fans with long memories, the contrast with the old days was stark.[6] In 1983, New South Welshman Les Boyd smashed his elbow into the jaw of Darryl Brohman, who was playing his first game for Queensland. Brohman fell to the ground and went into convulsions. In 1984, the second State of Origin game erupted into a free-for-all fight within seconds of the game's opening (smoke from the opening fireworks was still drifting across the field). In the second game of the 1988 season, an all-in brawl at Lang Park led to the referee sending off Queensland captain Wally Lewis. In 1991, Queenslander Mark Geyer started a fight in both the first half and the second half of the match.

What caused the League to 'get tough' on fights, declaring in 2013 that any player who punched an opponent would go to the sin bin for 10 minutes, regardless of the circumstances? The answer is that, as the cost to the NRL of fighting has gone up, Rugby League officials have seen to it that the supply of fights goes down. As teams have invested more in their players, the cost of an injured or suspended player has steadily risen. The likely risk of lawsuits by retired players has increased—with the American National Football League recently agreeing to pay US$765 million to 4500 former players for concussion-related injuries, similar lawsuits in Australia are all but certain. And the rise of AFL in New South Wales and Queensland creates a competitive threat to Rugby League: if parents don't like what they see on their screens, they're likely to turn the channel to another football code.[7] The result: fewer fights.

A young man playing Rugby League today is, in a sense, lucky—because he's significantly less likely to be punched on the field than in the 1980s. But that's just one of the many ways that luck affects sporting careers. An analysis of cricketers' performances compared two kinds of debuts: those whose first test match was a home game, and those who had their first test match overseas.[8] To the individual batsman, this is effectively random: anyone who gets a chance to play test cricket takes it immediately. Yet the challenge they face is quite different. For example, an Indian batsman will anticipate the cracks that often emerge on Indian pitches in the latter stages of a test match but might be utterly unprepared for Australia's bouncier wickets. On debut, a batsman who is playing at home scores one-third more runs—and the difference is persistent. If he is retained in the team, a home debut batsman has a career batting average one-fifth larger than a batsman who debuts overseas.

Our greatest batsman, Don Bradman, had plenty of good and bad luck in his career. He was lucky to debut in Australia, which gave him the chance to play his first game against England on an Australian wicket. Yet the English cricket team, under the captaincy of Douglas Jardine, responded to Australia's batting success by developing 'bodyline', a technique in which the ball was bowled towards the batsman's body along the line of the leg stump. In the 1932–33 season, a bodyline ball fractured the skull of Australian Bert Oldfield, and a rising ball struck the Australian captain Bill Woodfull under his heart, leaving him bent over in pain for several minutes. Approached afterwards by an apologetic English manager, Woodfull famously declared, 'There are two teams out there, one is playing cricket. The other is making no attempt to do so.'

In the short term, Bradman was regarded as being unlucky in facing bodyline. In the second test of the 1932–33 season, it had got him out on the first ball. Yet bodyline also had a long-term benefit for Bradman. As one biographer put it, 'Bodyline was specially prepared, nurtured for and expended on him and, in consequence, his technique underwent a change quicker than might have been the case with the passage of time. Bodyline plucked something vibrant from his art.' Ultimately, Bradman was perhaps lucky to have faced bodyline, because it made him a better batsman (which in turn makes you wonder whether Mitchell Johnson might inadvertently be creating the next English Bradman). Similarly, he was unlucky to have been at his peak when World War II forced the cancellation of four tests. Without the war, one economist estimated, Bradman's average would have been 100.74.[9]

As humans, we have a tendency to underplay the role of luck and overplay the role of skill. An economic study of soccer players looked at sports journalists' ratings of players who took a shot at goal and hit the post.[10] Imagine you could freeze the play (*Matrix*-style) at the moment the ball hits the post. Four-fifths of the time, the ball bounces off the post and goes out, while in one-fifth of cases it goes into the goal. You'd probably assume that all the players making these shots were pretty similar in ability, wouldn't you? Alas, soccer journalists rate players as being substantially more talented if the ball goes into the net than if it misses. Ultimately, some of the players aren't more skilled than their teammates, they're simply luckier.

But perhaps the biggest piece of luck you can have in sport is to be born in the right month of the year. To see this, imagine two players—Olivia and Emily—who both start playing soccer in primary school. Olivia is born in July, while Emily is born in August. Because the age cut-off for soccer is 1 August, Olivia starts playing as the youngest player in the under–8s team, while Emily plays as the oldest player in the under–7s team. Because of her age, Olivia struggles to keep up, while Emily is one of the biggest girls on the field. Olivia is the littlest on her team, and sometimes lets the side down. Conversely, Emily often gets the ball, and ends the year as the team's best scorer. The coaches do their best to nurture all the girls, but they love winning, and post-game talk often turns to Emily's natural talent. By the time the girls finish primary school, Olivia decides to drop soccer and play piano instead, while Emily becomes the captain of her school team.

Sound far-fetched? Let's look at the data. In Figure 1, I plot four distributions of birthdays across the year. First, I show the birthdays of everyone born in Australia in the 1980s. There is barely any difference between the least common month (February, which has fewer days, so only 7.9 per cent of births) and the most common month (March, with 8.8 per cent of births). Next, I look at three different sports: cricket, Rugby League and soccer. In each case, I show the distribution of birth-dates, along with the age cut-off that applied to most of the players I'm analysing. The cricket sample is all Sheffield Shield players (which includes the Australian team, plus those further down the ranks). The

Rugby League sample is all first-grade players. The soccer sample is those playing for the women's national team (the Matildas) and the men's national team (the Socceroos).[11]

For cricket, NRL and soccer, the notable feature about the graphs is the spike just to the right of the cut-off date.[12] This shows an excess of players who would have been among the oldest in their teams when playing age-graded sports. In cricket, the most common birth month is November (the third month after the cut-off), while in league and soccer the most common birth month for elite players is the month directly after the cut-off. A boy born in January is nearly twice as likely to play first-grade Rugby League as a boy born in December. A boy or girl born in August is more than twice as likely to play soccer for Australia than a child born in July.

Further evidence comes from changes in the cut-off. Until the late 1980s, the cut-off age for Australian youth soccer was 1 January. If you look at the distribution of top soccer players' birthdays in that era, the most common season of birth is the first few months of the year.[13] But when the cut-off date was shifted, the birthdates of top soccer players began shifting too. It's a fair bet that if we hadn't changed the cut-off age for youth soccer, the Matildas and the Socceroos would contain more members with January birthdays and fewer members with August birthdays.

The impact of chance on sporting careers reminds us of the ways in which good luck and bad luck affect all of our careers. Economic models that try to explain earnings based on

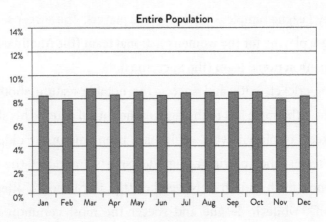

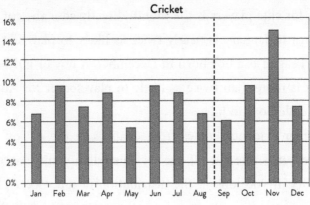

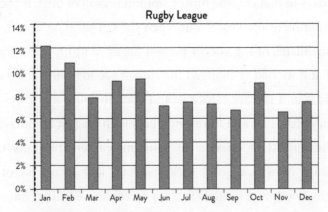

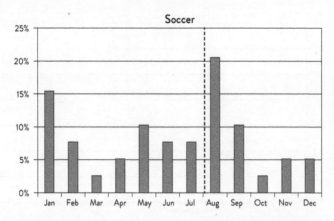

Figure 1: Can your birthday make you a sports star?

demographics only end up explaining about one-tenth of the differences between people. As for the other nine-tenths, a good deal of it is luck.

But you wouldn't believe me if I told you that money didn't matter in sport. Money allows teams to buy better players (up to the salary cap, if one applies), to hire better coaches and to buy experts like physiotherapists, masseurs and even statisticians.

To see the effect of money on team outcomes, let's take a look at AFL. In Figure 2, I added up the total amount each AFL club spent on its football programs (player salaries and other team expenses). I sum the amount teams spent over the five-year period 2008–2012, and then look at how this compared with the number of games the team won over the same period (I excluded Gold Coast and the GWS Giants since they were not part of the competition for the full five years). The line represents the average relationship between spending and success.

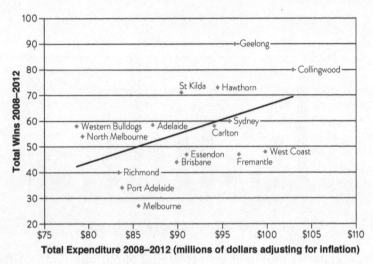

Figure 2: Spending and match wins in AFL

The first thing you notice is that there is generally a positive relationship. In the period 2008 to 2012, there were seven teams that spent less than $90 million: Western Bulldogs, North Melbourne, Richmond, Port Adelaide, Melbourne, Adelaide and Brisbane. All of them won fewer than 60 games in the five-year period, an average of fewer than 12 games in a 22-game season. At the other end of the spectrum, the biggest spending team was Collingwood, whose $103 million spend saw them win a total of 80 AFL games. On average, teams win one more game for every additional $1.1 million they spend.[14]

But the second thing you notice is that while some teams— like Sydney and Carlton—are clustered around the line, many are further away. Money accounts for about one-fifth of the variation between teams, but that leaves four-fifths to be explained by other factors. Geelong and Fremantle both spent about $62 million, but Geelong won 90 matches, while Fremantle won 47 games. St Kilda and Essendon both spent about $90 million, but St Kilda won 71 games, while Essendon won only 47 games.

Relative to their spending, the AFL teams that did best were Geelong (which won 28 more games than their expenditure would predict), St Kilda and the Western Bulldogs (both with 16 more games than their spending would predict). Those who under-performed their expenditure were Fremantle (who won 16 fewer games than their spending would predict), West Coast (18 fewer) and Melbourne (23 fewer). Economists like to talk about 'productivity', meaning how much you get out for what you put in. If you can sew twenty shirt buttons each hour, and I can only sew ten, we'd say you're twice as productive as I am. In these terms, the AFL's most productive team is Geelong (who also happened to pick up two premierships in this period), and the least productive team is Melbourne (who won the wooden spoon twice in this period). One possible reason for Geelong's success is the skill of its statistics-loving recruiter Stephen Wells, who has identified talent in unusual places, such as Mark Blicavs (an 800-metre runner with little background in the game when he was drafted in 2012) and James Podsiadly (drafted as a mature-aged rookie in 2010).[15]

Another area where money matters is the Olympics.[16] In Figure 3, I show the relationship between a country's national income and the number of medals they won at the 2012 Olympics. The top two countries on the medal tally are the world's two

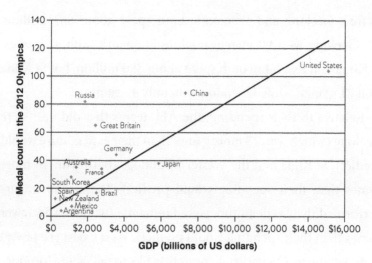

Figure 3: GDP and Olympic medals

biggest economies: the United States (104 medals) and China (88 medals). At the other end, there are 190-odd countries with a national income below US$1.5 trillion.[17] All of them won fewer than 40 Olympic medals.

The effect of money on Olympic outcomes is significant. For every additional $125 billion in GDP, a country wins on average one more medal.[18] To put this into perspective, $125 billion is about the value of the economic growth that Australia experienced between the Global Financial Crisis and the 2012 Games. During this period, Britain's economy failed to grow. If Australia's had also been stagnant, we could have expected one fewer medal in the 2012 games. But growth or no growth, it's clear from Figure 3 that Australia does significantly better at the Olympics than our economy would predict. For example, a nation with an economy the same size as ours would have been predicted to garner 16 medals. We won 35.

In the case of AFL, I was looking at actual sport spending figures by clubs. Here, the comparison is national income, so it omits the differences in how large a slice of the pie goes to sport. Yet while the AFL analysis only managed to explain one-fifth of the variation in results, the Olympic analysis succeeded in explaining more than two-thirds of the variation in medal counts. That's partly because richer nations are larger (and therefore have a bigger talent pool to choose their team from), but also because— unlike AFL—there's no attempt at equalisation in the Olympics.[19]

Indeed, international competitions are remarkably uncom- petitive. As Table 3 shows, if Australia and England were evenly balanced on the cricket pitch, then you would expect the outcomes from the 67 Ashes series that have taken place from 1882 to 2013 to look something like the results from a coin toss. Statistically, it turns out that if you toss a coin 67 times, you're unlikely to get a run of more than five heads or five tails. But in fact, there were two occasions in which Australia or England won (or retained) the Ashes more than five times in a row.[20]

International Rugby Union is similarly uncompetitive. Since 1931, there have been 54 series played between Australia and New Zealand in the Bledisloe Cup. If this were a game between two evenly matched teams, we wouldn't expect a run of successes longer than five years. There are two occasions on which a team's winning streak has exceeded this, including New Zealand's run

Table 3: How competitive are international and interstate sporting competitions?

Competition	Number of series	Longest run of wins if event competitive	Number of runs of wins exceeding this length
Ashes 1882–2013	67	5.1	2
Bledisloe Cup 1931–2013	54	4.8	2
State of Origin 1980–2013	34	4.1	2

of Bledisloe Cup victories from 2002 to 2013. The same is true of State of Origin Rugby League. From 1980 to 2013, there have been 34 Origin series. Statistically, you wouldn't expect a run of more than four series wins. But on two occasions there have been series in which Queensland won the State of Origin more than four times in a row.[21]

International cricket, international Rugby and State of Origin do hardly anything to help ensure the opposing teams are evenly matched. In this sense, they're quite different from many domestic sporting codes, which attempt to achieve what economists call 'competitive balance'. Underlying competitive balance is the idea that sports fans are more likely to enjoy a game where the outcome isn't quite so predictable. All sports fans like seeing their own team win, but we're more likely to stay in the stadium for a nail-biter than a walkover.

To achieve competitive balance, sporting officials have adopted a plethora of strategies. Television revenues can be shared out between teams, the total player salary bill can be capped, and a draft can allow the lowest-ranked teams to have the first pick of players. Not surprisingly, some clubs have attempted to breach these rules by breaking the salary cap or allegedly 'tanking' at the end of a season to get a better draft pick. But even so, the net result has been an improvement in the competitive balance of both AFL and Rugby League since the mid-1980s. Alas, sports economists are yet to reach a clear answer on which Australian football code is the more competitive.[22]

Having a fair referee also affects the competitiveness of a sport. Alas, several studies have shown that the 'one-eyed ref' is no fictional character. In cricket, Australian umpires are more likely to give a foreign player out lbw than an Australian player. In AFL, referees award more free kicks to teams from their home state. In international Super 14 Rugby Union, teams are more likely to win when the referee is of the same nation. In each of these cases, what seems to drive the bias is the size of the crowd. As the crowd dwindles, so does the 'home bias' of the referee. With a large crowd, the referee becomes more biased. One study that looked at video referees found that they were considerably less biased if they watched with the sound turned off.[23]

Indeed, some economic studies suggest that the only reason crowds matter at sporting events is via their effect on the referees.[24] When there's action on the field, the crowd always roars. At elite level, players are trained to draw inspiration as much from the growl of a hostile away crowd as the cheer of a supportive home crowd. But the threat of being yelled at by the home crowd does affect the behaviour of the referee. To avoid the disapproval of the fans, referees tend to make judgements that favour the home crowd. Foul calls and lbw decisions are surprisingly susceptible to the sound in the stadium. If you want to use your voice at a sporting match in the way that'll do most to change the result, just focus on shouting at the referee. But don't get too worked up . . .

In 2006, the World Cup was held in Germany. After the tournament, a team of Munich cardiologists analysed the pattern of heart attacks.[25] On days when the German team played, cardiac emergencies doubled for women and tripled for men. The increase was so dramatic that the researchers suggested fans with heart conditions might consider increasing their beta-blockers or having an extra aspirin on game days.

In a novel experiment, a team of psychologists tested testosterone levels among male Brazilian and Italian fans before and after the 1994 World Cup grand final.[26] Brazilian fans, whose team won after a penalty shoot-out, saw their testosterone levels rise. But Italian fans saw their testosterone levels drop. Individual sportsmen have been shown to get a testosterone boost from a win (and a testosterone slump from a loss). It seems that fans react in the same way.

As the saying goes, sport is not just a matter of life and death; it's much more important than that.[27] But much as we'd love to think that sport is all about skill, Lady Luck often intervenes. In a day–night cricket match, the team that wins the toss is 4 per cent more likely to win than the team that loses the toss.[28] And, as we've seen, individual careers are affected by luck in everything from the timing of when you're born to the timing of when you make your debut.

With its mix of competition and teamwork, high-stakes and high visibility, the sporting field turns out to be a valuable laboratory for testing many of the most interesting theories in economics: Which workers are the most productive? How does your first job affect your career? Do managers compare their employees in fair ways? Which firms make best use of their resources? How competitive is an industry? Sports economics helps shed light on these and many other crucial economic questions. As baseball great Yogi Berra said, 'You can observe a lot just by watching'.

Looking for a raise

Do women suffer more from glass ceilings or sticky floors, is it 'lookism' if handsome people earn more and does it pay to stay in school?

Matthew's mother was a skilled classical musician who struggled with mental illness and substance abuse. His father suffered from schizophrenia, and took his own life when Matthew (not his real name) was in primary school. By the time Matthew was a teenager, he was frequently skipping school, and left home at age fourteen. At the end of Year 10, he dropped out of school, and got a job at the local supermarket. There, he worked six days a week, earning just $5.70 an hour.

At that time, Matthew later told me, he realised that 'career prospects for someone in my position were exceptionally limited, but more importantly I always had a great love of learning and an appreciation for education, even though I never excelled at school'. Two years after dropping out, he found a school campus where he could return and study for Years 11 and 12. He received some financial assistance from the government, and the school provided counselling for the drug addiction and mental health problems that had begun to develop.

From Year 12, Matthew won a place at university. As he puts it, 'I also had a fair degree of luck', finding a job that allowed him to pay the bills, and that he could juggle around his study commitments. He stopped using drugs, and began building better relationships with those around him. A few years ago, he began his PhD in strategic studies. 'There was a time not long past', he told me, 'where just to be eating well and looking after myself would have been a victory. Thanks to the power of education, and a system that allowed me to access it, even on modest means and having made many mistakes, my life will never be the same again.'

This chapter applies economics to the world of work. The average Australian employee works 1728 hours every year, which means we're working for nearly one-third of our waking hours.[1] Work is the main source of income for most of us, and helps define our identity. How many times have you been in a conversation with a stranger where the opening question is 'So, what do you do?'

Some of the forces that affect what we get paid are predictable. As Matthew's story illustrates, one of these is education. Others—like height, weight and beauty—might surprise you. In this chapter, I'll illustrate some of the expected and unexpected factors that drive the Australian labour market, including the gender pay gap. And I'll look at why city-slickers earn more than their country cousins.

To begin, let's look at one of the big drivers of earnings: education. Average lifetime earnings are $1.7 million for a person who drops out of high school, compared with $2.1 million for someone who finishes Year 12. A diploma raises average lifetime earnings to $2.4 million, a bachelor's degree to $2.9 million, and a postgraduate qualification takes average earnings to $3.2 million.[2] In all probability, Matthew will earn twice as much in his lifetime as if he had not returned to education.

Economists think of education as an investment, with the main cost being forgone earnings. The biggest cost of studying at university isn't fees and textbooks; it's the fact that you're not able to work a full-time job (even those who work while studying, as Matthew did, generally opt for jobs that pay less and are more flexible). Non-economists often miss this aspect of education. If you don't pay cash for it, many people don't think of it as a 'cost'. But to an economist, something that reduces the amount of money coming into your purse is just as much an economic cost as something that increases the amount of money going out of your purse.

Like other investments, education involves a sacrifice now for a benefit later. In the case of education, better earnings aren't the only upside. When we look at people in their 40s and 50s, those with a degree have $540,000 more assets and are 9 per cent less likely to report a long-term health condition. And these differences really seem to be causal. When Melbourne University's Chris Ryan and I compared those who grew up in states with a higher school leaving age, we found that being forced to stay at school for an additional year boosted adult earnings by about one-tenth. Other researchers have reached similar conclusions.[3] Even for those who want to drop out of school, being *forced* to stay can bring benefits. As Woody Allen put it, '80 per cent of success is showing up'.

The good news for Australia is that, over the past generation, we've massively increased the average educational attainment of the population. Among those aged 25–34, 75 per cent have finished Year 12, 33 per cent have a vocational qualification, and 35 per cent have a university degree. The bad news is that we haven't been so good at raising quality. In one research paper, Chris Ryan and I went back to look at how junior high school students have done on answering the same question as their parents' generation. For example, the following question appeared on exams in both 1964 and 2003: 'Joe had three test scores of 78, 76, and 74, while Mary had scores of 72, 82, and 74. How did Joe's average compare with Mary's?'[4]

As you immediately worked out, both Joe and Mary have the same average. In 1964, 88 per cent of students answered the question correctly. In 2003, just 68 per cent answered correctly. The proportion of students able to correctly calculate an average dropped by 20 percentage points in four decades. In case you thought that things had picked up in the twenty-first century, evidence from the international PISA exam shows that Australian students' maths scores dropped from 2003 to 2012, while reading scores declined from 2000 to 2012.[5]

At best, literacy and numeracy scores of young Australians have flatlined over the past generation.[6] At worst, they've slumped. So while our nation is richer thanks to the rising *quantity* of education, we could benefit even more from an increase in the *quality* of our education.

Education is due partly to luck (of genetics, parents and circumstance) and partly to choice. But other aspects of the labour market are determined by luck alone. For example, if you eat properly as a child, your height is basically determined by your genes. But, when Southern Cross University researcher Michael Kortt and I looked at the relationship between height and wages, we found strong evidence that taller adults earn more.[7] For men, another 10 centimetres of height boosts wages by about 3 per cent (for a full-time worker on average wages, that's over $2000 per year). For women, another 10 centimetres of height boosts wages by nearly 2 per cent, which works out to $1000 a year for the average full-timer.

Understanding why height affects wages gives us a useful window into how economists think about labour market outcomes. One possibility is that height is a productive characteristic—in which taller workers are actually better at doing their job. For example, a taller shelf-packer might need to use the ladder less often, a taller firefighter might be able to reach a person in distress, and a taller police officer might carry a greater air of authority. But the other possibility is that tall people earn more not because they are more capable, but because of discrimination in their favour. In one study, Australian students were introduced to a man they were told was visiting from Cambridge University. Afterwards, they were asked to guess his height. Those who had been told he was a professor guessed that he was 5 centimetres taller than those who were told he was a student.[8]

If the results of British and US research carry over to Australia, then it seems most likely that the wage returns to height are a combination of discrimination and productivity.[9] In the case of men, what matters for their pay packets turns out to be not their adult height, but how tall they were as teenagers. Taller teens are more likely to engage in extracurricular activities, such as playing sports and joining social clubs. So if there is discrimination, most of it seems to be taking place at the high school level. By the time tall men hit the labour market, they really are more productive: the extra time spent in sporting and social activities has left them with better social skills than their shorter peers. (For women, the story is a little different—adult height seems to matter in its own right, not just through the channel of teen height.)

In other developed nations, researchers have found that slimmer people earned higher wages. Kortt and I found no such pattern in Australia, suggesting that being overweight might not have a large negative impact on people's ability to do their job effectively, and that perhaps there is relatively little discrimination against those who are carrying a few extra kilograms.

The other possibility is that people care about appearance, with body size just one dimension of the whole package. Put another way, do more beautiful people earn higher salaries? Testing this theory is harder than evaluating the impact of height and weight on wages. If you want to know the answer to that one, you only need to survey people by phone or mail. But if you want to know how good looking a person is, you need to meet them face-to-face.

My collaborator, Jeff Borland, is a labour economist at the University of Melbourne. I don't think he'd mind me admitting that neither of us has ever come close to making the 'Cleo's Most Eligible Bachelor' list. But we're both fascinated at understanding what drives differences in earnings, so we engaged one of the few market research companies that does face-to-face interviewing, Roy Morgan. After asking householders about their job and earnings, our interviewers were to write down whether they thought the person was more attractive, less attractive, or about as attractive as other people their age. Now, you might think that getting interviewers to rate beauty is inherently subjective but, like plenty of other researchers before us, we found that beauty is *not* in the eye of the beholder. When we asked our interviewers to rate the beauty of ten people in photographs, they came up with very similar responses.

With a few thousand responses, we set about analysing the patterns. As with the height study, we found that beauty mattered more to the employment outcomes of men than women. Good-looking men were more likely to have a job, and among those in employment, attractiveness was associated with higher wages. For both men and women, beauty also bought a higher-earning spouse. Overall, the effects were large and significant.

Men rated 'above average' for attractiveness had household incomes that were 15 per cent higher, while those rated 'below average' had household incomes that were 25 per cent lower. Put another way, Put another way, our raters put four in ten men into the above average beauty category, and one in ten into the below average category. The former had annual household incomes nearly $40,000 higher than the latter.[10]

Could this be due to productivity? Perhaps, but we don't find much evidence for it. Attractive people are not much more likely to be employed in a face-to-face occupation (such as sales) than an occupation that doesn't require meeting customers (such as manufacturing). In addition, when we hold constant self-confidence and intelligence, the beauty effect remains strong.

That leaves discrimination, or what you might call 'lookism'. From my assessment of the evidence, employers' favouritism towards beautiful workers looks more like prejudice than good management. There is nothing illegal about such discrimination in Australia, though a few US jurisdictions, such as Washington, DC, San Francisco and Santa Cruz do outlaw 'attractiveness discrimination'. If you (like me) are what novelist Jane Austen would have called 'plain', you have only yourself to blame if you attach a photograph to your CV and don't get an interview.[11]

While discriminating by looks is legal, gender discrimination has been officially outlawed for a generation. Yet gender pay gaps persist. One study followed people who change their gender through surgery and hormone therapy.[12] For those who switched from female to male, wages rose, and many reported a rise in respect and job opportunities. For those who switched from male to female, wages fell, and it was common to report a loss of authority and an increase in harassment. These were literally the same individuals, but when their gender changed, so did their earnings.

Four in every ten Australian workers are women, but their hourly wages are 17 per cent lower than men's. In the private sector, the gender pay gap is 8 per cent for low-paid workers, but 28 per cent for high-paid workers. A similar pattern seems to hold in many other developed nations.[13] To an economist, the question is: how much of this is due to differences in productivity, and how much is due to discrimination? Put another way, if it was the case that women were earning less solely because they had less labour market experience, then we probably wouldn't think the employer was behaving badly (though we might look at the societal factors that led to the experience gap). But if an employer was hiring men and women with the same qualifications and experience, yet paying men more, then we would likely conclude discrimination was to blame.

Holding constant a raft of factors—from experience and education to union membership and industry—researchers Juan Barón (Central Bank of Colombia) and Deborah Cobb-Clark (Melbourne Institute) looked at the extent to which productivity-related characteristics explained the gender pay gap for low-paid, medium-paid and high-paid women working in the private sector.[14] For low-paid women, the gender pay gap is entirely explained by productivity-related traits (particularly experience). For medium-paid women, three-quarters can be explained by such characteristics. For high-paid women, less than one-quarter of the gender pay gap is due to differences in productivity-related characteristics. As the researchers put it, 'the issue seems to be one of glass ceilings rather than sticky floors'.

This finding matches the results of a mischievous experiment conducted by Australian National University researcher Alison Booth and myself.[15] We devised fake CVs, differing only in the names at the top of the page, and set about applying for entry-level jobs in four industries: waitstaff, data entry, customer service and sales. The CVs were identical, but the names changed, so one firm might receive a CV from Sarah Mitchell, while another got a CV from Brian Johnson. We found discrimination in *favour* of female applicants applying for low-paid jobs, with the typical female name receiving a callback 32 per cent of the time, compared with 25 per cent for the typical male name. For jobs at the bottom of the labour market—which are often traditionally female—women have a better shot than men at getting a foot in the door.

But things are different at the top. Women comprise just 12 per cent of ASX200 board directors and 4 per cent of CEOs. Only 9 per cent of senior barristers are women, and one quarter of university professors. Asked about gender barriers in the law, one female lawyer described 'a culture fostering a "harden up" approach that you are weak if you don't want to work ridiculous hours'. Another noted that the workplace rewarded 'aggressive behaviours (rather than positive, teaching behaviours)'.[16]

Noticing that women seem to be particularly unrepresented in high-stakes environments, economists have turned to look at attitudes to competition. One experiment asked male and female university students to solve straightforward mathematical problems.[17] When paid a flat rate for every correct answer, men and women did equally well. Students were then given the chance to enter a four-person tournament, in which the top-ranked player won a handsome prize, and everyone else got nothing. Since men and women had similar ability, they stood a similar chance of sweeping the pool—but it turned out that men were twice as likely to enter the tournament as women.

Other studies suggest that gendered attitudes to competition emerge at a young age. When nine-year-old school children in Israel were timed running a short sprint on their own, boys and girls did equally well.[18] When they were paired up and asked to race against another student, boys ran faster. But girls ran equally fast in a race as they did on their own.

Could these results represent an evolutionary norm, in which the genetic advantage lies with competitive males and cautious females?[19] Or do the differences have more to do with culture and upbringing than innate biological differences?

One way to separate the hypotheses is to look at extremely different societies. One of the most innovative tests involved economists carrying out the same experiment in an extremely patriarchal society (the Maasai in Tanzania) and a matrilineal society (the Khasi in India).[20] The task in this case was throwing a ball into a bucket placed some distance away. In both societies, men and women were equally accurate. Then they were given a choice: they could either be paid $1 for each ball that went in the bucket, or enter a competition with an (unidentified) person behind the building, in which the most accurate thrower won $3 per ball, and the other person got nothing. Among the patriarchal Maasai—a society where women are 'treated like donkeys'—men were more likely to compete than women. But in the matrilineal Khasi society—where authority positions and property rights are held by women—women were more inclined to compete than men. In fact, Khasi women turned out to be more competitive than Maasai men. Score: nature 0, nurture 1.

Another way to see the effect of context on competitiveness is to look at sex-segregated education. In two experiments involving British 15-year-olds, researchers tested students' willingness to enter a competition that involved skill (solving mazes), and another competition that involved luck (tossing a coin).[21] When the experiments were carried out with boys and girls from coeducational schools, girls were less likely to enter either competition. But girls from single-sex schools were just as willing to compete as coed boys.

Alison Booth, one of the leading researchers in this field, is quick to point out that 'our research should not be interpreted as saying that we should all immediately enrol our daughters in single-sex schools'.[22] But the study does suggest that context matters. If the stereotype that girls are averse to competition can be broken by something as simple as single-sex schooling, it should be possible to change it in other ways too. Indeed, one study found that women who read biographies of successful women did significantly better on a subsequent maths test.[23] In economic terms, reducing discrimination requires focusing on both the demand side (by stamping out workplace discrimination) and the supply side (by encouraging women to develop a more positive attitude to competition—or perhaps endeavouring to make men less competitive).

It's worth recalling that we're focusing on averages. There are low-paid women who suffer severe discrimination, and high-paid women who are paid the same as their male counterparts. Just because the pay gap at the bottom of the wage distribution is explained by workers' characteristics, it doesn't follow that all is well with the world. It just means that among low-wage workers, the gender pay gap is largely due to the fact that women do most of the child-rearing.

Gender discrimination can show up not only in pay differences, but also in sexual harassment. In a 2012 survey, a quarter of Australian working women reported that they had been sexually harassed in the previous five years. International studies suggest that up to half of all women will be sexually harassed at work at some point in their career.[24] Not only is sexual harassment wrong in itself, it is also likely to damage women's careers: for example, by making women more reluctant to ask for a pay rise and more likely to quit. Economics hasn't had much to say about the causes of sexual harassment, and hasn't yet offered innovative ideas to reduce its prevalence. I hope that changes soon.

Lastly, let's look at the effect of the place you live on how much you earn. Australians have long romanced the bush. Banjo Paterson's 1889 poem 'Clancy of the Overflow' contrasts a drover who 'sees the vision splendid of the sunlit plains extended' with an urbanite, who must endure 'the foetid air and gritty of the dusty, dirty city'.

And yet it was in the following year that economist Alfred Marshall wrote perhaps the most famous economic defence of cities. In a city, Marshall argued:

> *The mysteries of the trade become no mysteries; but are as it were in the air, and children learn many of them unconsciously. Good work is rightly appreciated, inventions and improvements in machinery, in processes and the general organization of the business have their merits promptly discussed: if one man starts a new idea, it is taken up by others and combined with suggestions of their own; and thus it becomes the source of further new ideas.*[25]

To test the effect of city living on wages, I looked at an Australian survey that has followed around 20,000 people for more than a decade. During this time, some of the people in the survey have moved from the bush to the city, while others have gone in the opposite direction, so the survey allowed me to observe the wages of the same person working in two different locations.

On average, moving from a rural area to a big city is associated with an 8 per cent increase in annual income.[26] Much of this effect seems to be driven by average levels of education. Holding constant a person's own income, a 10 percentage point increase in the proportion of the working age population with university degrees is associated with a 5 per cent rise in income.[27] For example, if a person moves from rural Queensland (where 14 per cent of the working age population have a university degree) to Sydney (where 35 per cent of the working age population have a university degree), we can expect their income to increase by more than 10 per cent.

Analysing this effect in the United States, Harvard's Ed Glaeser found that city-dwellers earn significantly more, even after taking prices into account.[28] Workers in cities are more productive, and their wages rise faster over time. This isn't because city dwellers are smarter (in fact, in the United States, IQs are higher for people born in rural areas), but largely because urban workers acquire job skills at a more rapid rate. It's easier to find the perfect employer–employee match in a big city, and it's simpler to start a business. On average, those who opt for 'the sunlit plains extended' over 'the dusty, dirty city' will earn about $200,000 less over their career.[29] But because cost of living differences in Australia are large, they will spend less too.[30]

In my view, understanding the labour market is one of the most interesting aspects of economics. As with most areas of life, the answer is a mix of fairness and unfairness. Moving to a city or poring over a textbook has a significant pay-off. But so does being born tall or beautiful. In fact, not only do beautiful people earn more, they are also more effective in collecting charitable donations and perform better on television game shows. Beautiful people are less likely to become criminals, and if they do end up in a courtroom, beautiful defendants are less likely to be convicted.[31]

As is well known, women tend to earn less than men—but what is striking is the fact that this is driven more by gender gaps in high-paid occupations (such as lawyers) than in low-paid occupations (such as hairdressers). And I haven't even had space to touch on a plethora of other labour economics findings, such as the fact that employee share-ownership plans boost productivity, union members earn more, gay men tend to earn less, and job-seekers with non-Anglo names get fewer callbacks.[32]

For the most part, what I've focused on in this chapter has been a snapshot of the labour market. But as well as comparing ourselves with other people, we also want to think about how our earnings will progress over our life cycle. Let's see what economics has to say about when we might reach our peak.

Careering through life

What can we learn from the career cycles of great artists and why did Sidney Nolan, Regurgitator and Markus Zusak peak younger than Arthur Boyd, Nick Cave and Kate Grenville?

Einstein's major contributions to physics were published when he was aged 26. At the same age, Picasso produced one of the seminal paintings in modern art. Mark Zuckerberg launched Facebook at age 19. Mathematician Terence Tao won the Fields Medal (maths' Nobel Prize) at age 31.

At the other end of the life cycle, examples also abound. Clint Eastwood won an Oscar for *Unforgiven*, directed when he was 62, and another for *Million Dollar Baby*, directed at age 74. Paul Cézanne's most valuable work was painted in the year of his death, aged 67. Frank Lloyd Wright began designing the Guggenheim Museum when he was 76, and finished when he was aged 91.

Planning a career isn't easy, because (unless you believe in reincarnation) you only get one shot at it. On average, most of us get paid less when we start out. This is partly because we're still learning our roles and partly because we're looking to find the job that's right for us. Young people typically change jobs more frequently. Like a single in the dating market, a young worker is looking to figure out the best 'match'. This typically involves switching employers—and sometimes even careers. The longer we work, the more experience we accumulate. Problems start to look more familiar, we have more perspective in dealing with troublesome customers and co-workers, and we have a better understanding of the organisation we're working with.

But at the same time as we're accumulating experience, we're losing brain function. Over time, our brains shrink, DNA damage accumulates, and brain 'plasticity' declines. Each decade from our twenties to our nineties, we become less proficient at tasks such as remembering lists of words or classifying shapes.[1] Are you aged over twenty? If someone asks you to take an IQ test, don't delay—it's likely you'll do worse in a year's time.

So our productivity is a function of two things: rising experience and falling cognitive power. Put these together and the wages of the average Australian worker peak around age 50. And yet we all know people who (like Einstein) did their best work early on, and those who (like Clint Eastwood) seem to get more savvy with age.

This chapter is about success over the life cycle, answering the question: why do some people peak early and others bloom late? For many of us, it's hard to precisely work out our peak, so I'm going to look at creative geniuses—painters, musicians and novelists—whose careers are well documented.

Admittedly, the question of life cycles throws up its own challenges. You can't be a late-bloomer if you don't live a long life (I'm reminded of the 37-year old comedian who once quipped, 'When Mozart was my age, he had been dead for two years'). And the model applies most clearly to men, because women have traditionally taken longer career breaks when they have children. What follows are some initial ideas about creative life cycles in Australia, rather than the last word on the topic.

In analysing artistic careers, I'm going to borrow a toolkit from the world's leading authority on the economics of creative innovation: University of Chicago economist David Galenson. Over more than a decade, Galenson and his co-authors have studied the careers of economists, poets, novelists, directors, architects and artists. To identify the stars of each field, he gathers empirical data: rankings of 'all-time greats', auction prices, prizes, citations, and the number of times works appear in textbooks and anthologies. Studying a large volume of data, he looks for patterns that hold right across the spectrum of creative endeavour.

Studying artists has the advantage that we not only have ready measures for success, but also can delve into biographies to learn something about the creative process of individuals. I find Galenson's work fascinating not only because of what it says about particular artists, but also because it offers a new way of thinking about when each of us is likely to peak in our jobs.

Across a diverse set of fields, Galenson claimed to have consistently identified two types of innovators: 'conceptual' innovators, whose work implements a single theory, and 'experimental' innovators, whose work evolves from real-life experience and empirical observation. Conceptualists are often interested in imagination and fantasy, while experimentalists tend to focus on describing and observing reality. Because it's easier to know your own ideas than it is to comprehend the world, conceptualists tend to be surer at an early age of what they want to show or say. Accordingly, conceptual innovators often do their best work at an earlier age than experimental innovators.

In art, Galenson distinguishes conceptual artists (Raphael, Pablo Picasso, Edvard Munch) whose work aimed to communicate specific ideas and emotions, from experimental artists (Leonardo da Vinci, Paul Cézanne, Vasili Kandinsky) whose ideas were vaguer and who often regarded the artistic process as a journey. Experimentalist Cézanne once said: 'I seek in painting.' Conceptualist Picasso said: 'I don't seek; I find'.[2]

Art auction prices show the difference in the careers of Picasso and Cézanne. Paintings by Picasso in his twenties are worth four times as much as work done in his sixties. But experimentalist Cézanne continued to improve: work he did in his sixties sells for fifteen times as much as paintings from his twenties.[3]

Galenson takes the same ideas to novelists. Here, conceptualists have specific goals, and are best known for their plots (F. Scott Fitzgerald, Ernest Hemingway). Experimentalists are more focused on character development (Charles Dickens, Virginia Woolf). Again, we see the same age pattern: Fitzgerald wrote *The Great Gatsby* at age 29, while Dickens—drawing on tougher life experiences—wrote *Bleak House* at age 41. An obituary of conceptualist Hemingway bluntly stated: 'Most of his late work was bad, Papa gone soft'.[4]

And then there's poetry. Galenson argues that conceptualists (e e cummings, T.S. Eliot) are technically sophisticated and grounded in literary history, while experimentalists (Wallace Stevens, Robert Frost) draw more from ordinary speech and observation. Conceptual poet T.S. Eliot penned 'The Love Song of J. Alfred Prufrock' at age 23. By contrast, nearly half of Stevens' best poems were written after age 50. At age 63, he described his late works as more important than his early ones 'because, as one grows older, one's objectives become clearer'.[5]

We can also look at movie directors. Galenson argues that conceptualists (Orson Welles, Stanley Kubrick) are those whose movies were carefully planned and animated by single ideas. Experimentalists (Alfred Hitchcock, Woody Allen) were generally less sure of their goals, and often made major changes to a movie during shooting. Welles was just 26 years old when he directed and starred in *Citizen Kane*. Hitchcock was 59 when he directed *Vertigo*, followed two years later by *Psycho*. As one critic wrote, 'Hitchcock's mastery of the art grows greater with each film'.[6]

Galenson's research is fascinating for those concerned with creative endeavour by Europeans and Americans. But to an Australian, the question remains: to what extent does the framework of young conceptualists and old experimentalists apply to our artists? To test this, I set about crunching data and reading biographies in three categories of creative endeavour: Australian painting, Australian rock music and Australian novel-writing.

Let's start with Australian painters. To compile a list of the top Australian artists, we could either look at art auction prices, or ask the experts. As an economist, I'd intuitively prefer to use auction results, but because they are only available since the 1980s, they simply don't capture many of the top nineteenth-century artists.[7] (The masterworks of late nineteenth-century painters were mostly hanging in public galleries by the 1980s.) So, instead, I plumped for expert opinion. Taking three of the best-known compendiums of Australian art, I added up the number of works by each artist.

In rank order, the top ten Australian artists are Tom Roberts, Arthur Streeton, William Dobell, Arthur Boyd, Russell Drysdale, Charles Conder, Frederick McCubbin, George Lambert, Sidney Nolan and David Davies. Table 4 separates these artists into conceptualists and experimentalists, and lists the age at which they painted their most famous work.[8] Remember that from about age twenty, our raw cognitive power is declining, while our experience steadily increases. So we would expect conceptualists (whose work is based on a single idea) to peak at an earlier age than experimentalists (whose work draws on their life experiences). On average, the conceptualists did their best painting at age 28, while the experimentalist painters peaked at age 37.

Among the conceptualists, the principal group are five 'Heidelberg School' artists: Tom Roberts, Arthur Streeton, Frederick McCubbin, David Davies and Charles Conder. Formed in the

Table 4: Career cycles of painters

Artist	Top painting and age when created
Conceptualists	
Tom Roberts	*Shearing the Rams* (34)
Arthur Streeton	*Fire's On! Lapstone Tunnel* (24)
Frederick McCubbin	*Down on His Luck* (34)
David Davies	*Moonrise, Templestowe* (30)
Charles Conder	*The Departure of the S.S. Orient* (20)
Sidney Nolan	First Ned Kelly Series (28 to 30)
George Lambert	*A Bush Idyll* (23)
Average peak age of conceptualists: 27.7	
Experimentalists	
Arthur Boyd	Bride Series (35 to 38)
William Dobell	*The Irish Youth* (39)
Russell Drysdale	*Sofala* (35)
Average peak age of experimentalists: 36.8	

late 1880s, the Heidelberg School focused around a specific goal: accurately depicting the Australian landscape. Like the French impressionists, they painted outdoors (*en plein air*), and sought to capture the harsh sunlight and earthier colours of the Australian bush. Many of the works of the Heidelberg School were small, with some finished in as little as half an hour. As Tom Roberts put it: 'Painting fixes one thing for you, one scene, one mood, one idea.'[9]

Roberts, Streeton, McCubbin, Davies and Conder did their best work when they were aged in their twenties and thirties.

Indeed, Conder produced his best-known painting, *The Departure of the SS* Orient, the year before joining the school, aged just nineteen. Streeton wasn't much older when he reached his peak, painting his finest works in his early twenties. Art critic Robert Hughes argued, 'Streeton's vision expanded not a whit in the last 40 years of his life.' Another critic pointed out that the Streeton works that appreciated most in value after his death were those painted when he was aged in his twenties.[10]

Another conceptualist is Sidney Nolan, whose iconic Ned Kelly images are perhaps the most dominant single idea in Australian art. In the early 1940s, Nolan was involved with the Angry Penguins, a modernist movement inspired by European surrealism and expressionism. Produced shortly after the end of World War II, the Kelly images flowed out of Nolan's fascination with the bushranger story, coupled with his own personal circumstances. Nolan had gone absent without leave from the army, and was having an affair with a married woman. As Nolan told one interviewer, 'Really the Kelly paintings are secretly about myself'.[11]

The Kelly paintings were done when Nolan was in his twenties, and his work never again reached such heights. As critic Robert Nelson argued, 'the long period from [age 33] to Nolan's death [at age 75] reveals a painter who identified with nothing, whose stock-in-trade was painting subjects in which he showed no belief'. Similarly, George Lambert painted his most famous work, *A Bush Idyll*, at age 23. He turned to portraiture, but as one biographer noted of works produced when he was in his late forties, they 'tend to reflect with their increasingly dry colour and muted characterisation an increasing disenchantment'.[12]

By contrast, Arthur Boyd was an experimentalist, greatly influenced by the Australian landscape. His travels with Indigenous communities in Central Australia inspired his *Bride* series, while the Vietnam War and Boyd's interest in biblical stories led to his *Nebuchadnezzar* series. Social movements affected Boyd's art too. For example, he was one of the first Australian artists to express the theme of racism against Indigenous people.

Critic Robert Hughes has described Boyd's sense of art as 'a kind of tribal wisdom, an inheritance ceaselessly modified'.[13] Hughes also notes Boyd's 'steady, consistent development', which led to him being commissioned in his mid-sixties to design a tapestry for the Great Hall of Parliament House. Like Picasso and Cézanne, Nolan and Boyd overlapped in their careers, but while Picasso and Nolan peaked young, Cézanne and Boyd continued to improve with age.

Two other key Australian experimentalist painters were Sydney artists William Dobell and Russell Drysdale. Dobell—argued Robert Hughes—'remained fundamentally eclectic', influenced by Renoir, Goya, Soutine, Rembrandt and Daumier.[14] His pictures moved from the grotesque to the elongated, and his 1943 Archibald Prize–winning portrait of Joshua Smith was so distorted that a group of fellow artists challenged the prize in court on the basis that it was a caricature, not a portrait. (Dobell won.)

Drysdale drew his sources directly from the environment. Some of his paintings show the influence of fleeting European fashions—such as cubism, surrealism and social realism. But Robert Hughes argued that his experience of travelling in the Australian outback meant that Drysdale helped '[pull] Australian landscape from the limbo of fleece and gum-tree in which it had lain stiffening for thirty years'. Hughes also credited Drysdale with being one of the first to make Indigenous Australians a major theme of his art—a result of Drysdale's extensive travels in northern Australia.[15]

An all-time great list will invariably be biased towards dead white men. I'd like to think that a future researcher could replicate this exercise in a century's time and come up with a list of names that were more representative of the gender and ethnic diversity of today's Australia. But in the meantime, it's worth saying something about how our leading Aboriginal artists might be categorised.

In general, Australia's greatest Indigenous artists appear to have been experimentalists. Kimberley artist Rover Thomas worked as a stockman droving cattle for the first part of his life, and did not begin painting until he was in his fifties. Thomas drew heavily on his life experiences. He was, as one commentator put it, 'consciously re-tracing not only his own intimate knowledge of hill, valley, homestead, dry creek bed and swollen rivers. In his mind and in his canvases, he [was], simultaneously, re-living a personal and group history'.[16]

Similarly, Western Desert artist Clifford Possum Tjapaltjarri produced his most famous painting *Warlugulong* at age 45.

Trained as a wood-carver, he continued to adapt his dot paintings, eventually abandoning a brush for the chewed-off end of a stick. Likewise, a biographer of Hermannsburg School artist Albert Namatjira noted that he always painted 'with country in mind', and drew on ancestral associations.[17] Namatjira's most famous watercolours, such as *Ghost Gum* and *Across the Plain to St Giles*, were produced when he was in his forties and fifties.

Northern Territory artist Emily Kame Kngwarreye did not begin painting on canvas until her late 70s, producing over 3000 paintings during her eight-year career. If we're fortunate enough to live into our 70s, all of us will find ourselves less able to solve complex mental problems. What we have instead is a deep reservoir of experience. So if Kngwarreye had been a conceptualist, it's unlikely her work at this age would have been appealing. What made her a success was that she was an experimentalist. As an Anmatyerre elder, Kngwarreye's subjects were the cultural connections that her community had with the country. Kngwarreye's experimentalist approach can be seen in the way she drew on her lifetime of work on pastoral properties and camel teams, to paint what she called 'whole lot'.[18]

Now, let's look at rock musicians. Since album sales data are patchy, I compiled a list of all-time best Australian bands from three different lists: a prominent book on all-time best Australian albums, a survey of 175 music industry experts, and a survey of Triple J listeners. Each source provided its 100 'best' albums, which I combined into a single list of bands.[19] In rank order, the top ten Australian bands are Midnight Oil, Silverchair, Nick Cave and the Bad Seeds, Powderfinger, AC/DC, You Am I, Crowded House, INXS, Regurgitator, and Cold Chisel. Like the list of top painters, it's a male-dominated list.

Table 5 splits the bands into conceptualists and experimentalists. For each band, I've shown their top album, and the age of the main songwriter when the album hit the stands.

Perhaps the most internationally influential Australian band on the list is AC/DC, formed in 1973 by brothers Angus and

Table 5: Career cycles of rock musicians

Band	Top album and age of main songwriter when released
Conceptualists	
AC/DC	*Back in Black* (33)
Crowded House	*Woodface* (33)
You Am I	*Hi Fi Way* (26)
Silverchair	*Frogstomp* (15)
Regurgitator	*Unit* (25)
INXS	*Kick* (28)
Average peak age of conceptualists: 26.7	
Experimentalists	
Midnight Oil	*Diesel and Dust* (34)
Cold Chisel	*East* (24)
Nick Cave and the Bad Seeds	*The Boatman's Call* (40)
Powderfinger	*Odyssey Number Five* (31)
Average peak age of experimentalists: 32.3	

Malcolm Young. From 1975 to 1985, the band averaged an album a year. I have classified them as conceptualists because their riffing style and 'stadium-rock dramatics' remained the driving idea behind the band's music.[20] For many bands, the loss of a lead singer might shift its style, but Bon Scott's death in 1980 seems to have had little impact on AC/DC's approach. The confidence that the band knew who they were is reflected in an interview with Angus Young about the introduction that Malcolm Young had written for *Back in Black*: '[Malcolm] said "what do you think of that? Is it rubbish? Should I trash it?" So I said "No, don't trash it. If you're going to trash it, give it to me and I'll say I wrote it!"'[21]

Another conceptualist band is Crowded House (which Australians have claimed as one of ours ever since they shot to stardom). Although members of Crowded House came and went, the band's musical ethos was driven by Neil Finn, who had been influenced by Maori music, Irish folk music and his brother Tim's band Split Enz. Neil Finn had a strong confidence in the ideas he was seeking to convey in his music. For example, describing 'All I Ask', from the album *Woodface*, Neil Finn told one interviewer: '"All I Ask" was written in one go, literally as long as it takes to sing it was as long as it took to write it.' His brother Tim added 'We only ever did it once. We played it and sang it and recorded it without any percussion whatsoever and played it back and went, "yeah, that's a song".' (The comment echoes Bob Dylan, who once told an interviewer: 'Just about as much time as it takes to write it down is about as long as it takes to write it.')[22]

Conceptualist bands tend to hit their peak early. Silverchair's best-rated album was *Frogstomp*, produced when the band members were aged fifteen (which led to them being dubbed variously 'Silverhighchair' and 'Nirvana in Pyjamas'). Regurgitator's top album was *Unit*, the second album they released. A look at the top chart ratings for INXS show clearly the band's cycle: their first two albums peaked at 27th and 15th. Then came seven albums that reached the top 10. INXS's last three albums have peaked at 14th, 18th and 49th respectively. By contrast, experimentalist band Powderfinger continues to produce albums that peak at number one.

On the experimentalist end of the spectrum lies Midnight Oil. From its inception, Midnight Oil not only changed its name (the band was originally called 'Farm'), but also its entire lyrical focus. Late 1970s Midnight Oil songs focused on losing love and catching waves, leading music critic Bruce Elder to describe their music as 'sexist, secular and bigoted'.[23] Over the course of the next decade, the focus of the songs shifted to nuclear disarmament, the US alliance and Indigenous reconciliation. In contrast with Crowded House's 'one-take' recording, Midnight Oil would spend months rehearsing songs to get them just right. As songwriter Jim Moginie put it, 'We wanted to get all the fat out of the songs. Simplicity was the key.'[24]

Cold Chisel took a similar approach, using performances in industrial cities such as Wollongong and Newcastle as a chance to develop songs. As Jimmy Barnes described their experimental style, 'We scrapped all of our arrangements . . . if Ian wanted to play five verses of a guitar solo, he just went up the front and did it and if I wanted to sing for longer, I did it. It was a really loose, free-form thing, we were developing and changing the songs every night to suit the atmosphere we were in'.[25]

Perhaps the classic experimentalist in Australian music is Nick Cave, whose music draws on the Old Testament, outlaw stories and Gothic imagery. Cave's style changes from album to album, and his top-rated album, *The Boatman's Call*, was released when he was 40 years old. He has also experimented with a startling array of other artistic media, training as a painter in his late-teens, and writing screenplays, poems, novels and a comic book. In a 1988 interview, Cave said 'My ideas are self-generating now, they spring from what I've done before. . . . I don't think I'm fully formed or ever will be, but my basic creative journey is now self-perpetuating'.[26]

In 2013, Nick Cave's album *Push the Sky Away* became the first album he had ever had at number one in Australia. He was 55.[27] This reflects the overall picture from the music industry. As the data from Table 5 show, conceptual musicians peak on average at age 27, while experimental musicians peak on average at age 32.

Now, let's look at novelists. Again, I've combined three lists of top Australian novels: a popular poll conducted among viewers of the ABC television program 'First Tuesday Book Club', a membership survey by the Australian Society of Authors, and a survey conducted by Booktopia (which describes itself as 'The No. 1 Book Blog for Australia').[28] This approach relies less on expert wisdom than do the lists of leading painters and musicians, and doubtless some may quibble with the results. But as with the other creative careers, my main focus is less on the overall ranking than on differentiating conceptualists and experimentalists among Australian novelists.

In order, the top ten Australian authors are: Patrick White, Tim Winton, Peter Carey, David Malouf, Norman Lindsay, Ruth Park, Christina Stead, Kate Grenville, Markus Zusak and Joan Lindsay. Table 6 splits these novelists into conceptualists and experimentalists, and shows the age when they produced their top-ranked book. On average, conceptualists published their best book at age 39, while experimentalists published theirs at age 46.

In general, conceptual novelists tend to be plot-driven, with more extensive use of symbols. Running through Markus Zusak's *The Book Thief* is the story of Liesel Meminger, who was born in Germany in the 1920s and died in modern-day Sydney. Rather than striving for precise historical accuracy, Zusak uses the technique of having the story narrated by Death (who turns out to be afraid of people). In one interview, Zusak noted that the idea for the story came from two powerful images: a burning sky after a city has been bombed, and a passer-by being punished for giving bread to a starving Jewish man. With these images, and the idea of a fearful Death, Zusak says, 'I started writing and I didn't stop.'[29] The title not only evokes the theft of a literal book, but also is a metaphor for Hitler's use of words to launch the Holocaust.[30]

Table 6: Career cycles of novelists

Author	Top book and age when published
Conceptualists	
Markus Zusak	*The Book Thief* (30)
David Malouf	*An Imaginary Life* (44)
Patrick White	*Voss* (45)
Christina Stead	*The Man Who Loved Children* (38)
Average peak age of conceptualists: 39.3	
Experimentalists	
Kate Grenville	*The Secret River* (55)
Tim Winton	*Cloudstreet* (31)
Ruth Park	*The Harp in the South* (31)
Peter Carey	*True History of the Kelly Gang* (57)
Joan Lindsay	*Picnic at Hanging Rock* (71)
Norman Lindsay	*The Magic Pudding* (39)
Average peak age of experimentalists: 47.3	

Similarly, Christina Stead's work delves into the psychology of family life, focusing more on the structure of that internal sphere than external events. *The Man Who Loved Children* features a narcissistic patriarch who creates his own language for the family—and a daughter who responds by inventing her own code. The outside world matters so little that Stead was able to acquiesce to her publisher's suggestion that the book would sell better if it were set in Washington DC rather than Sydney.[31] As critics have pointed out, symbols are significant in Stead's work.[32]

Two other conceptualists are Patrick White and David Malouf, who opened up a new space in male writing to focus on issues of identity, loneliness and belonging. As Malouf told one interviewer, 'An awful lot of Australian male writing, and Australian writing about men, was about the world of action. I don't think that was ever an accurate depiction of men's lives.'[33] For both men, their sexuality—and the experience of coming of age in an Australia where homosexual acts were illegal—helped to forge their writing. White's writing style is another clue to his conceptualist approach. While experimental writers often make their most important discoveries during the writing process, conceptualists are more likely to formulate their ideas before writing. Describing Patrick White's original manuscripts, biographer David Marr wrote: 'He scratches out paragraphs here and there, but essentially the prose rolls out in a long, clean ribbon. Characters, scenes and dialogue emerge fully formed.'[34]

Although her greatest novel was published when she was in her early thirties, Ruth Park, in style, is closer to an experimentalist. The focus of *The Harp in the South* and *Poor Man's Orange* is principally on the memorable characters of the Darcy family, not on the plot itself (indeed, the same holds for the *Muddle-headed Wombat* series). Describing Park's writing style, one commentator described her 'Dickensian quest for the odd and the comedic'. Park herself referred to the importance of 'characters who must, absolutely must, walk, talk and think for themselves'. Describing what makes her work special, Park observes 'The world is full of novels in which the characters simply *say* and *do*. There are certainly legitimate genres in which this is sufficient. But in real and lasting writing the character *is*.'[35]

The goal of depicting characters in a realistic manner has led some experimental authors to extremes. For example, Kate Grenville's research is so detailed that her most famous book, *The Secret River*, was accompanied by a companion book (*Searching for the Secret River*) that detailed the historical research. In *The Lieutenant*, Grenville created a rule for herself that the only lines of dialogue she would use would be those that appeared in the original notebooks of First Fleet soldier William Dawes.[36] As is the case with other experimentalists, characters rather than plot dominate Grenville's writing. In one interview, she baldly declared 'Stephen King says that plot is the last resort of the mediocre writers, and I think he's right'. She also noted that her characters evolve during the writing process: 'I usually start off with a broad idea of a character but it undergoes a gradual morphing over the period of writing.'[37]

Another experimentalist, Peter Carey, drew on history and the natural environment for his inspiration. Among his novels are works inspired by the Kelly gang (*True History of the Kelly Gang*) and French political thinker Alexis de Tocqueville (*Parrot and Olivier in America*). It is perhaps no accident that Carey has written a novel inspired by one of the works of another experimentalist, Charles Dickens (*Jack Maggs* is a reworking of *Great Expectations*). As with Grenville, Carey peaked later in life, winning the Booker Prize at age 45 (and again at age 58). While conceptual novelists like Joyce and Fitzgerald sometimes do their best work in their twenties, it is an age when experimentalists are often just finding their voice. Carey wrote five novels in his twenties but none of these was ever published.

Both Joan Lindsay and Norman Lindsay are characterised by a diversity of creative output. Joan Lindsay trained as a painter, shifting to writing only after her marriage. She wrote short stories, plays and non-fiction works, and only published her masterwork, *Picnic at Hanging Rock*, at the age of 71.[38] Norman Lindsay, like Nick Cave, worked across a startlingly broad array of art forms. In his forties, he would reportedly draw a watercolour before breakfast, produce etchings until mid-afternoon, work on a concrete sculpture until dinner, and in the evening write a chapter for his latest novel. Norman Lindsay's writing was exploratory rather than emerging fully formed: *The Magic Pudding* was written as a way of distracting himself from the horror of World War I, in which his brother was killed.[39]

Lastly, there's Tim Winton, whose most popular book so far, *Cloudstreet*, is ranked number one on all three lists. The natural environment is fundamental to Winton's novels, which are grounded in real places along the Western Australian coastline. As he put it, 'The place comes first. If the place isn't interesting to me then I can't feel it. I can't feel any people in it. I can't feel what the people are on about or likely to get up to.' His storylines are enjoyable, but the books are fundamentally about the evolution of his characters. These characters sometimes overlap between stories, as with Queenie Cookson in *Shallows* and *Breath*. As Winton puts it: 'I've always enjoyed that these people lean on the door and suddenly they are in the set of another book.'[40] (A similar pattern can be seen in the Mississippi novels of William Faulkner, another experimentalist.)

Describing his writing style, Winton says 'I don't start with a plan or a plot or anything. I just start with a few little flickers, you know, and just wait and see what they end up being.' He notes that his approach to writing is to show up at the desk, work 'union hours', and hope that the ideas flow. *Dirt Music*, Winton says, was inspired by 'a couple of scraps of imagery, a naked man embracing a boab tree, a woman stepping into the body of a guitar.'[41] The stories are strongly autobiographical: as one character in *The Turning* observes, 'every vivid experience comes from your adolescence'.

Beyond painting, music and novels, the Galenson approach could be applied to other fields of creative endeavour in Australia. In poetry, Kenneth Slessor is a conceptualist, while Les Murray is an experimentalist. Among fashion designers, Collette Dinnigan is a conceptualist, while Lisa Ho is an experimentalist. Among architects, Jørn Utzon is a conceptualist, while Walter Burley Griffin is an experimentalist. Indeed, a recent analysis has even applied the dichotomy to scientific endeavour, showing that among Nobel laureates in medicine, chemistry and physics, conceptualists peak earlier than experimentalists.[42]

As the saying goes, there are two kinds of people in the world: some who believe the world can be divided into two kinds of people and some who believe it's more complicated than that. Sure, the Galenson approach doesn't perfectly sum up the creative process, but it does provide insights into why some people peak early and others bloom late. Perhaps you even see yourself in one of these two creative approaches. Are you a conceptualist or an experimentalist? And what does that mean for whether you're likely to be below or above your peak performance age?

6

Cops and dollars

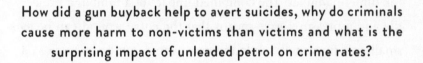

How did a gun buyback help to avert suicides, why do criminals cause more harm to non-victims than victims and what is the surprising impact of unleaded petrol on crime rates?

When economists study crime, we think about incentives: how easy is it to commit a crime, what are the chances of getting caught and what is the penalty? In this chapter, you'll read about the impacts of conventional crime reduction strategies such as more police and longer jail sentences, and less conventional ones such as better schooling, more effective prisons and abortion law reform. But let's start off with two of the most shocking crime stories in Australia, the policy that they led to and its unexpected effect.

On the chilly Melbourne evening of Sunday 9 August 1987, 19-year-old former army cadet Julian Knight drank several beers at the Royal Hotel in Clifton Hill, then packed a bag with an M14 semi-automatic, a Ruger 10/22 semi-automatic, and a Mossberg pump action 12-gauge shotgun. As he later told the police, 'I wanted to see what it was like to kill someone'.[1]

Most bullets are less than a centimetre wide, but when they enter a person's body, the hole they make is far larger. One reason for this is that, once inside your body, a bullet begins to 'yaw', or tumble.[2] Because bullets are a few centimetres long, the tumbling effect is far more destructive than if the bullet had continued to travel in a straight line. In addition, a cushion of air known as a 'pressure wave' precedes the bullet, temporarily creating a cavity inside the body that can be much wider than the trajectory of the tumbling bullet. The combined impact of a tumbling projectile and a pressure wave means that the entry wound can be as small as a fingernail, while the exit wound can be as large as a tennis ball.

Bullets cause death in a variety of different ways. Since the heart is the body's pump, a direct hit from a bullet causes catastrophic blood loss. If a bullet strikes the head, it typically destroys so much of the brain tissue that the brain can no longer function (the effect of the pressure wave is far more destructive in the head than in the chest cavity). If the bullet hits a major internal organ or a central artery, loss of blood can cause death over a few minutes. If the bullet perforates the lung, the victim can suffer a pneumothorax, with death eventually caused by a lack of oxygen in the bloodstream. Bullets are even deadly in the abdominal cavity, where they can lead to death by septicaemia.

Taking up a concealed position on the corner of Ramsden Street, Knight started firing at people driving down Hoddle Street. He managed to hit several cars, injuring passengers but initially not killing anyone. Among those wounded were Vesna Markovska and her fiancé Zoran Trajceski, who stopped their cars nearby. Then Knight shot at a car containing Kevin and Tracey Skinner, and their son Adam. Tracey was hit in the face and killed.

Shortly afterwards, Vesna Markovska stepped away from her car, and was spotted and shot by Knight, who then shot her twice more while she lay on the roadway. As Robert Mitchell came over to help her, he too was shot and killed. A minute later Gina Papaioannou attempted to assist, and was fatally shot.

Knight next shot another passing driver, Dusan Flajnik, who bled to death in his car. Shortly afterwards, motorcyclist Kenneth 'Shane' Stanton was shot in the leg by Knight. As he lay on the ground writhing in pain, Knight shot Stanton repeatedly. As Knight later told interviewers, 'I didn't want to keep him in . . . any more agony, so I let off another three rounds until he stopped screaming'.

By the time Julian Knight was captured by police—about 45 minutes after he started shooting—he had fired more than 100 rounds of ammunition. Seven people had been killed, and nineteen others seriously injured.

Julian Knight is my adopted second cousin. I've never met him.

Nine years after the Hoddle Street Massacre, on Sunday, 28 April 1996, Tasmanian man Martin Bryant put into the boot of his car a Colt AR-15 semi-automatic rifle, an FN FAL semi-automatic rifle, and a Daewoo 12-gauge shotgun.[3] At a guesthouse, he shot and killed an elderly couple, who had had a family dispute with Bryant's father. He then drove to the Port Arthur tourist site, and entered the Broad Arrow cafe, carrying the AR-15 rifle inside a blue sports bag. Inside the cafe, Bryant ordered a large meal, ate quickly, then opened his sports bag. Almost immediately, he shot two Malaysian visitors, Moh Yee Ng and Soo Leng Chung, then moved through the crowded cafe, shooting rapidly. The first twelve victims were shot within fifteen seconds. By the time Bryant left the cafe, he had killed twenty people and injured another twelve. He then continued shooting tourists around the coaches parked at the car park, before getting in his own car and driving back out of the site.

Walking up the hill to get away, Nanette Mikac came within sight of the toll booth that marked the entry to the park, and said to her six-year-old daughter Alannah, 'We're safe now, Pumpkin'. Then a car stopped next to her and Bryant got out. Placing a hand on her shoulder, Bryant asked Nanette to get down on her knees. Her last words before he shot her were 'please don't hurt my babies'. Bryant then shot three-year-old Madeline. Alannah tried to hide behind a tree, and Bryant shot at her twice, missing both times. He then walked up and pressed the rifle against her neck before firing.

At the toll booth, Bryant murdered four more people, and took their car. Then at a service station near the toll booth, he met his final two victims: 28-year-old lawyer Zoe Hall and her companion Glen Pears.

I was a summer clerk at the law firm where Zoe worked, and she was my mentor.

In the wake of the Port Arthur massacre, newly elected Prime Minister John Howard worked with state and territory governments to implement tougher gun regulations. One of the strongest advocates was Walter Mikac, whose wife and two daughters had been murdered by Bryant. Addressing a rally of 3000 people in the Sydney Domain, he said 'As you know, three months ago to this day, I lost the entire reason for my existence'.

To make sure that the tougher rules actually reduced the number of weapons, they were also accompanied by a buyback program. From mid-1996 to mid-1997, anyone could take a gun to their local police station, and the police would pay its fair value. In total, nearly 650,000 weapons were handed in to police. While some of these were weapons that had newly become illegal (pump-action shotguns and semi-automatic rifles), many people seem to have simply taken the chance to 'clean out the closet' by handing in weapons that were legal if the owner had an appropriate licence (such as .22 rifles). In the Northern Territory, police even paid compensation for a set of World War II aircraft cannons. According to one survey, the proportion of Australian households that had at least one gun dropped from 15 per cent to 8 per cent as a result of the buyback.[4]

Did the buyback save lives? As someone with a connection to two of Australia's worst gun massacres, I've always been interested in finding out. But the public debate seemed frustratingly simplistic. Some anti-gun campaigners described firearms owners as 'gun nuts', and seemed to have difficulty understanding how anyone could enjoy gun collecting, target shooting or hunting. Conversely, gun-rights advocates would say things like 'guns don't kill people, people do', which doesn't take the debate very far, given that the same can be said for fragmentation grenades, poison gas and surface-to-air missiles.

With Christine Neill, an expatriate Australian now living in Canada, I set about analysing data on the buyback. One result was rock solid. In the decade before the gun buyback, Australia averaged more than one mass shooting per year (a mass shooting is where five or more people are killed). Between 1987 and 1996, a total of 94 victims were killed in mass shootings. Apart from Hoddle Street and Port Arthur, there were also mass shootings in the Top End (Northern Territory and Western Australia), Canley Vale (New South Wales), Queen Street (Victoria), Oenpelli (Northern Territory), Surry Hills (New South Wales), Strathfield (New South Wales), Terrigal (New South Wales), Cangai (New South Wales) and Hillcrest (Queensland).[5]

In the decade after the laws were changed, there was not a single mass shooting in Australia. The chance of this change being due to luck alone is less than 1 in 100.[6] Judged by whether it prevented mass shootings, the Australian gun buyback was an unmitigated success. Yet impressive though this is, the number of people killed in mass shootings has never been particularly large. Even during the worst period for gun massacres, the odds of being killed in a mass shooting were about as large as the chances of being killed by a lightning strike.[7]

Neill and I then set about looking at other types of gun deaths. We learnt that the person most likely to kill you with a gun is yourself. The next most likely person to kill you with a gun is your spouse. The next most likely people to kill you are household members, relatives and acquaintances. You are least likely to be killed by a complete stranger. So we decided to look at the impact of the gun buyback on the overall firearm homicide and firearm suicide rates.

We approached the question in two ways. First, we looked at national trends. We found that—notwithstanding the mass shootings—gun homicide and gun suicide rates had been steadily falling for nearly two decades before the buyback. Some fancy statistical analysis seemed to suggest that the buyback had caused the firearm homicide and suicide rates to fall a little faster, but it was difficult to be sure, so we tried another approach.

In some states, the number of firearms per person that were bought back was larger than in other parts of Australia. We asked the question a little differently: did places with more gun buy-backs experience a larger drop in gun homicide and suicide? The answer turned out to be a resounding yes. For example, in the case of firearm suicide, the greatest reduction in weapons occurred in Tasmania, which was also the jurisdiction that saw the biggest drop in firearm suicide. Meanwhile, the smallest reduction in firearms per person was in Canberra, which also had the smallest drop in the firearm suicide rate. We did not find evidence of a corresponding increase in other forms of homicide (such as knife killings) or suicide (such as self-poisoning). Overall, we estimated that the Australian gun buyback saved at least 200 lives per year—mostly suicides.[8]

But the buyback had been expensive. Around half a billion dollars in compensation was paid to gun owners. Was it worth it or would Australia have been better off putting the money into other lifesaving measures, such as safer roads or better hospitals? To answer this question, we need a way of valuing gun deaths in monetary terms. For non-economists, this is sometimes regarded as a ghastly exercise: how can we put a dollar figure on a life? But for economists, having an estimate of the value of a statistical life helps us decide when a life-saving measure is cost-effective. By looking at how much people are willing to pay for health care and safety measures, economists are able to come up with a figure for the value of a 'statistical life'.

The value of a statistical life most commonly used by Australian policy-makers is $2.5 million.[9] On this basis, the economic value of saving 200 lives a year is around half a billion dollars, so the economic value of the gun buyback every year is about the

same as the one-off cost paid in 1996–1997. Since it was imple-
mented, the gun buyback has paid for itself more than ten times
over. And the vast bulk of the benefit came not from reduced
mass shootings, but from an entirely unexpected source: fewer
gun suicides.

While relatively few people die from mass shootings, the fear
generated by the Port Arthur massacre should not be ignored. It
is true that Australia probably lost as many people to road accidents in the week after the Port Arthur massacre as died on that
tragic Sunday.[10] But that simple analysis ignores the fact that fear
of crime imposes a real cost on the community.

It was the nineteenth-century philosopher Jeremy Bentham
who first argued that crime might have an impact on non-
victims. A violent crime, Bentham suggested, did a 'primary
mischief' to its victim but it also caused a 'secondary mischief'.
As reports circulated, people would go out of their way to avoid
the spot where it happened. Some might spend money to protect
themselves. Others could be too scared to leave their homes at all.
Bentham reminded us that the ripples of crime spread out well
beyond the event itself.

Fear of crime isn't always proportional to the risk of crime. For
example, women tend to be most fearful of violent crime, yet men
are most at risk.[11] We probably all know friends whom we think
are too worried about crime. Perhaps because people's worries
don't always match the true danger, the economics of crime has
largely ignored fear.

To help fill the research gap, I carried out a study with British economist Francesca Cornaglia and US economist Naomi Feldman.[12] In essence, we aimed to test Bentham's theory in Australia. Matching up surveys of mental wellbeing with data on police crime reports, we found that an increase in crime was associated with lower levels of mental wellbeing for people who were not a victim of any crime. When crime surged, people in the neighbourhood who hadn't been victims tended to experience more emotional problems, nervousness and depression. Moreover, we found that media reports of crime act as a 'multiplier'—causing crime to have an even larger negative impact on mental wellbeing.

This finding suggests that crime is yet more serious than we might have thought. As a community, we've always known that we need to cut crime to protect the man who might be assaulted, the family whose house might be broken into, and the woman whose car may be stolen. We also know now that we need to cut crime so that families can continue to let their children walk to school, women can go jogging at dusk and older people can feel safe catching the train.

To understand what drives crime, let's start by looking at crime rates in Australia over recent decades. Ideally, we would look at a wide range of crimes, but shifting definitions and changes in reporting rates have made long-term trends unreliable for some offences (for example, domestic violence is more often reported than in the past). So I'll focus on the one crime that has the fewest problems in reporting: homicide.

From the end of World War II, Australia's homicide rate climbed steadily—from an annual rate of around 1 per 100,000 in the 1940s to a peak of 2.4 per 100,000 in 1988. Thereafter, it slowly declined, staying below 2 people per 100,000 throughout the 1990s. In the most recent figures, the homicide rate was just above 1 person per 100,000. Your chance of being a victim of homicide in the late 2000s was around half of what it had been in the late 1980s.

What caused the drop? One of the lessons of economics is that government policies often have unintended effects, so let's start with two crime-reduction strategies you've probably never heard about: legalised abortion and unleaded petrol.

The evidence for both effects originates in the United States, where crime has followed a similar pattern to Australia. In the case of legalised abortion, the story starts in 1973 when the US Supreme Court decision in *Roe v Wade* effectively legalised abortion, leading to a dramatic increase in the number of terminations performed. The turning point in violent crime in the 1990s coincided with the period when children born in the post–*Roe v Wade* era would be reaching their late teens, and crime continued to fall as this generation reached the peak ages for criminal activity. Moreover, the handful of US states that legalised abortion before *Roe v Wade* were also the first to witness a fall in crime. Researchers John Donohue (Stanford University) and Steven Levitt (University of Chicago) concluded that legalised abortion accounted for a significant share of the drop in US crime rates.[13]

When Justin Wolfers and I read the study, we decided to test the theory on Australia.[14] Although Australian crime data aren't as good as US figures, we found some similar trends. While there is no single *Roe v Wade*–type decision in Australia, a number of seminal changes can be identified. Court decisions in Victoria in 1969 and New South Wales and the ACT in 1971 substantially broadened the circumstances in which abortions could be legally performed. Legislative changes in South Australia in 1969 and the Northern Territory in 1974 had a similar effect.

The changes did not occur in every jurisdiction. In Tasmania, Queensland and Western Australia, the legal status of abortion remained unclear throughout the 1970s. But, for more than two-thirds of the Australian population, the change occurred in the late 1960s or early 1970s—or about twenty years before the drop in crime rates. Wolfers and I also found some evidence that the drop in homicide occurred first in the states that legalised abortion the earliest.

The reaction to the two sets of findings could not have been more different. In the US, Donohue and Levitt earned the opprobrium of both those who are Pro-Life (who thought the researchers were arguing that the murder of a million foetuses could be offset by 6500 fewer homicides) and those who are Pro-Choice (who thought the researchers were suggesting that we could weed out society's villains in the womb). In Australia, the publication of my research with Wolfers garnered a single letter to the newspaper.

Now that the dust has settled, it's worth noting that legalised abortion has only a minor effect on the number of children brought into the world—its main effect is to change *when* they are born. Thus, the main effect is not that families have fewer children, but rather that all of these children are born when the parents feel ready to raise them.[15] In *Freakonomics*, Levitt (writing with Stephen Dubner) argued 'when the government gives a woman the opportunity to make her own decision about abortion, she generally does a good job of figuring out if she is in a position to raise the baby well. If she decides she can't, she often chooses the abortion.'[16]

The other major cause of the crime drop was unleaded petrol. In the 1920s, fuel companies began adding lead to petrol to improve performance. At the time, people knew that high quantities of lead could cause poisoning, but didn't realise that even small amounts of lead can be harmful—particularly for children. Several research papers have found that children with moderately high levels of lead in their blood are more hyperactive, impulsive and easily distracted. With difficulty controlling their behaviour, children who have more exposure to lead are more likely to commit crimes as adults. Lead exposure increases the chance of ADHD and it boosts the chance of children having a low IQ, a predictor of committing crimes later in life. Although children can also ingest lead from house paint, leaded paints were largely phased out in the 1950s and 1960s, leaving leaded petrol as the largest risk to children.

In a careful analysis of the US experience, Jessica Wolpaw Reyes of Amherst College uses the fact that the *Clean Air Act* phased out lead from petrol over the period 1975 to 1985, but did so differentially across states.[17] When Reyes analysed the changes in violent crime two decades later, she observed that the drop in crime was sharpest in the states that were first to reduce their lead levels. Moreover, the effect is independent of the change in abortion laws, which happened at a similar time, but did not perfectly coincide with the drop in lead levels.

In Australia, the phase-out of leaded petrol did not start until 1986, but took place at the same time nationwide (preventing me from replicating Reyes' cross-state comparison for Australia).[18] Yet if we assume that the impact on crime was similar in both countries, it suggests that unleaded petrol might have been responsible for reductions in crime in Australia as late as the mid-2000s. Tragically, Reyes' results also suggest that if Australian policymakers had banned leaded petrol when their US counterparts did, then tens of thousands of children may have grown up with better life chances, and thousands of crimes might have been averted.

So far, we've talked about three factors that affected crime in surprising ways. The gun buyback reduced firearms deaths: but mostly through fewer domestic shootings and suicides, not by its effect on reducing mass murders. In the case of abortion laws, the reduction in crime came because these laws helped women bear children when they felt ready to raise them. And unleaded petrol dramatically reduced young children's exposure to a substance that we now know is associated with impaired brain development.

Political debates about crime aren't generally focused on these more distant causes. When that well-known state candidate Laura Norder is on the ballot paper, it's typically because voters want more police on the streets and more criminals in jail. So let's review what we know about the way that policing and punishment affect crime.

According to the leading economic studies on the issue, both police officers and imprisonment cut crime. Police numbers affect crime because the more police there are on the beat, the higher the probability that a criminal will get caught. For every 10 per cent increase in police numbers, crime rates fall about 4 per cent. Yet although the number of Australian police officers per person rose in the 1970s, it hasn't changed much since then.[19] So it stands to reason that police numbers cannot be a major driver of the drop in violent crime over recent decades.

Incarceration reduces crime through two channels: deterrence and incapacitation. Deterrence works because would-be criminals look at those behind bars and decide not to commit an offence. Incapacitation works because while you're locked up, you can't commit a crime (more specifically, you can't commit a crime on the general population). Like sports players, criminals tend to have short careers, peaking in their late teens and early twenties. So if you lock up criminals for a few years, you dramatically reduce their lifetime propensity to commit violent crimes. Overall, every 10 per cent increase in the prison population cuts crime by around 3 per cent.[20]

Yet while prisons reduce crime in the short term, there are major concerns over their long-run effect on society. Over recent decades, Australia has invested in building prisons at an astonishing rate. In 1991, the national imprisonment rate was 117 prisoners per 100,000 adults. By 2013, it had risen to 170 prisoners per 100,000 adults. Each prisoner costs the taxpayer nearly $300 per day—about the price of a nice hotel room in a big city.[21]

The story is even worse for Indigenous Australians. When the *Indigenous Deaths in Custody Report* was released in 1991, there was widespread shock at the level of Indigenous incarceration in Australia, at 1739 prisoners per 100,000 Indigenous adults. Yet over the next two decades the Indigenous incarceration rate increased even further. In 2013, 2336 out of every 100,000 Indigenous adults were behind bars.[22] In Western Australia, 4 per cent of all Indigenous people are currently in jail. Even adjusting for the fact that Indigenous people tend to be younger, they are still fifteen times more likely to be in jail than non-Indigenous people. By their mid-20s, 40 per cent of Indigenous men have been formally charged by police with a crime.[23]

For the most part, the growth in Australia's prison population has been driven not by a rise in crime (indeed, many measures of crime have fallen), but by law changes, such as tougher bail conditions and mandatory non-parole periods.[24] Longer sentences have an incapacitation effect, but probably not much influence on deterrence. Increasing sentence lengths from five to ten years may sound tough, but if you are dealing with someone who lives from day to day—or, in economic jargon, a person with a high discount rate—it could have no effect on crime rates. The certainty of the punishment matters more than its size.[25]

The United States spells out in chilling terms what could lie ahead for Australia if we keep locking more and more people up. US jails currently hold over 2 million people, more than 1 per cent of the adult population. Among men aged 20–34 who did not complete high school, the US imprisonment rate is a jaw-dropping 12 per cent for whites and 37 per cent for blacks. And that is just the proportion behind bars on any given day. If you are an African-American man who does not finish high school, the odds are two in three that you will see the inside of a prison cell by the time you reach your mid-30s.[26] Young black men in the United States are now more likely to go to jail than to serve in the military or graduate from a four-year university degree.

Extremely high incarceration rates raise the risk that jails become less of a place for rehabilitation than a hotbed for breeding better criminals. The median sentence length in Australia is three years, so released prisoners find it hard to get a job and often discover that the only friends who have not deserted them are the ones they made inside. Sexual violence in prison is probably not as common as in the 1990s—when New South Wales magistrate David Heil-pern estimated that one-quarter of young male prisoners were raped—but the rate is likely higher than in the outside world.[27]

A large prison population also means that more children have a parent in the lock-up. Although we don't have good surveys of prisoners' children, a rough rule of thumb is that there are about as many children of prisoners as there are prisoners. That means about 30,000 Australian children have a parent behind bars. And although there are organisations that work specifically with children of prisoners, we know that children with a parent in jail are more likely to commit crimes themselves.[28]

What else might help cut crime? To answer this question, let's take a quick look at the early lives of some of Australia's most infamous criminals.

Mick Gatto is one of the few survivors of Melbourne's gangland wars and has served two terms in jail. According to his autobiography, Gatto began his life of crime at 'six or seven' by stealing from family, friends, 'pinball machines rigged for gambling' and even the firemen whose station was next door to his house. He used the money to rig more pinball machines and became more adventurous at stealing. Gatto became known as the 'devil of South Melbourne'. By the time he was thirteen, Gatto had been expelled from several schools, was constantly 'belted' by his father, and had found himself in trouble with police. Gatto recalled that the 'truant officer' told his father 'his schooldays are finished. He's got to start work.'[29]

Dropping out of formal education is a common theme in criminal lives. Notorious Sydney gang-rapist Bilal Skaf left school at age fourteen. Convicted murderer Neddy Smith wrote in his autobiography that he last saw the inside of a classroom at age thirteen. Port Arthur murderer Martin Bryant could not read or write when he left school. The typical prisoner has fewer than ten years of education—substantially below the general population.[30] Once behind bars, they have little chance of improving their schooling. Fewer than one-third of prisoners are engaged in any formal education program.[31]

Careful economic research has established a causal link between good education programs and less crime. Most famously, the Perry Preschool program in the 1960s showed that children who had received high-quality childcare at ages three to five were half as likely to have been arrested by age 27. Another randomised experiment demonstrated that children who attended a better quality school were half as likely to have been arrested over the next few years.[32] Both these studies support the old adage that building great schools now saves building prisons later. Because crime has such a high social cost, quality schools and early childhood centres in disadvantaged communities are a bargain for society at large.

The evidence on education illustrates a broader point about successful crime reduction strategies: we should be innovative in devising solutions, open to the possibility that the best approaches may not be traditional ones, and scientific and critical in assessing what works. When I lived in Sydney, one of the people I most liked to listen to on the radio was Don Weatherburn, head of the Bureau of Crime Statistics and Research. In a debate often dominated by ideologues, Weatherburn's calm voice and his reasoned appeal to numbers felt like a cool breeze on a hot summer afternoon. I also enjoyed the fact that he was prepared to admit when he wasn't sure whether a particular crime policy helped or hurt.

Using this same evidence-based philosophy, a team of researchers at the Washington State Institute of Public Policy looked at 571 evaluations of anti-crime policies. Among the programs that they found to have the largest effect were prevention programs such as nurse–family partnerships and high-quality early childhood programs targeted at very disadvantaged families. For juveniles, education programs and aggression replacement training were effective, while the 'Scared Straight' program actually *increased* offending. For adults, vocational training and programs for offenders with mental illness were particularly effective.[33]

Others have argued for a variety of novel policies, including changing the hours of high school from 9 a.m. to 3 p.m. to 11 a.m. to 5 p.m., short but mandatory jail stays for parole violations, better enforcement of warrants, and using concentrated enforcement as a response to gang killings.[34]There is also evidence that for some offences, restorative justice makes victims feel better and reduces overall crime levels.[35]

It's also worth thinking about the perverse incentives created by the current contracts that Australian states write with private prison providers. These bear a remarkable similarity to sheep agistment contracts. Providers are penalised if inmates harm themselves or others, and providers are rewarded if they do the paperwork correctly. We know that prisons are often less a portal to a new life than a revolving door. Of the 20,000 or so people who are released from jail each year, around half will have returned in the next two years. Yet private prison contracts say nothing about life after release. A prison operator receives the same remuneration regardless of whether released inmates lead healthy and productive lives—or become serial killers. That's an odd set of incentives.

To an economist, a smarter way to run private jails would be to contract for the outcomes that matter most.[36] For example, why not pay bonus payments for every prisoner who does not re-offend? Surely a private prison operator who teaches generosity, empathy and life skills deserves to get more money from the government than one who runs what a Hollywood movie famously called an 'Animal Factory'? Indeed, private prisons could even be paid in proportion to the amount that inmates legally earn after release. Given the right incentives, private prisons might even be able to teach the public sector a few lessons on how to run a great rehabilitation program.

When I was 22, I clashed with Bob Carr over the issue of criminal justice. Carr, then leader of the New South Wales state opposition, had complained publicly about gangs roaming the streets of Sydney, 'their baseball caps turned back to front'. As a Labor candidate in the 1995 New South Wales election, I spoke at the state ALP conference—wearing a baseball cap turned back to front. My argument was that a tough-on-crime strategy ends up incarcerating the poor. Carr's argument was that it is the poor who are most likely to be victims of crime. Both arguments are correct. While we can point to examples of white-collar crime, most offences involve a low-income victim and a low-income perpetrator. If you care about reducing hard-core poverty, you should be interested in smarter criminal justice policies.

In this chapter, I've looked at some unexpected policies that drove the fall in crime over recent decades. Introduced to stem mass shootings, the gun buyback had its biggest effect in reducing domestic firearms killings (and averting gun suicides). Similarly, legalised abortion and unleaded petrol had a major impact on reducing crime in ensuing decades.

Yet today, too much of our criminal justice debate is stuck in the 'tough on crime' rut. While it is true that locking up more people does reduce crime in the short run, it also has a long-run cost in the form of unskilled ex-cons and children damaged by their fathers' incarceration. What crime policy needs today are more innovative ideas, and the willingness to rigorously evaluate them. On the early evidence, education may be the best crime-fighting tool around.

At age 21, Michael Coutts-Trotter was jailed for conspiring to import half a kilogram of narcotics.[37] He was addicted to heroin, and lucky not to have overdosed, been shot or contracted AIDS from the people whose needles he had shared in Darlinghurst. Entering jail, he weighed about 40 kilograms, and was 'psychotic from lack of drugs and lack of sleep'. Over the next three years, he rotated through maximum-security jails, including Long Bay, Bathurst and Parramatta.

Two decades later, Coutts-Trotter was appointed Director-General of the New South Wales Department of Education. He had spent a year in a Salvation Army program after his release from jail, and then worked for senior politician Michael Egan. Former prisoner Bernie Matthews said Coutts-Trotter 'has become a role model to those still behind the walls and razor wire of state prisons . . . one of the very few whose sheer guts and determination successfully defeated the vicious cycle of prison-parole-and-more-prison'. After a change in state government in 2011, the Coalition retained him as a senior public servant.[38]

Getting criminal justice policy right is not easy, but if there is one country that can lead the way, it should be Australia: the nation that showed the world that if they are given a chance, ex-prisoners can do just as well as anyone.

7

Helping the world's poor

Why do poverty, corruption and terrorism go together, how does the Olympics crowd out Third World tragedies and can the idea of comparative advantage apply to foreign aid?

Jaqueline Lima was born homeless in Campinas, Brazil, in 1989.[1] Her mother, Irinèia, was 21 years old when Jacqueline was born. Irinèia was an alcoholic, and Jaqueline was her fourth child; the children had three different fathers. For the first seven years of Jaqueline's life, she lived on the streets. When Jaqueline was seven her aunt took her into a rehabilitation clinic for women alcoholics and drug addicts. There, Jaqueline found out that she was HIV positive.

The clinic provided Jaqueline with anti-retroviral drugs, and at age ten she began attending school for the first time in her life. Initially, she was very careful not to tell other pupils about her illness, but eventually she confided in one of her classmates. Jaqueline's trust in her friend was misplaced. As she put it: 'The next day, everyone knew I had AIDS.'

Seizing the moment, her teacher asked Jaqueline to do a report for the class on sexually transmitted diseases. It helped her regain a sense of self-belief, and led to her involvement in national networks of young people with HIV and AIDS.

Working as a waitress after school, Jaqueline shared a kiss one night at a bus-stop with one of her co-workers. She told him: 'I have a disease. I have AIDS'. Laughing, he replied: 'I love you, Jacky! I love you!' Jaqueline felt like fireworks were going off around her.

Together, they decided to have a child. It was risky but something they both desired. The doctor adjusted Jaqueline's drug cocktail and her son was born HIV negative. Jaqueline said, 'My hope is that children like Heitor will not cease to be born.'

Even a single dose of anti-retrovirals, administered at the time of the birth, dramatically reduces the chance that a pregnant woman will pass HIV on to her child. Yet in the two decades between Jaqueline's birth and Heitor's birth, the world moved from a situation in which virtually no women in developing countries received anti-retroviral treatments to one in which anti-retrovirals were given to more than half of all women at the time their children are born. Without foreign aid, this would have been impossible.

Jaqueline told her story in São Paulo, Brazil, at a conference I was attending for the Global Fund to Fight AIDS, Tuberculosis and Malaria. Established a bit over a decade ago, the Global Fund reflects the hope that rich countries might unite to tackle three of the worst diseases that humankind has ever faced. It now accounts for most of the global spending on tuberculosis and malaria, and a fifth of the world's spending on HIV/AIDS.

The creation of the Global Fund also signals frustration. Over the past half-century, developed countries have spent more than $2 trillion on foreign aid—around the total annual income of Italy. Yet many of the countries that have received the most aid have the least to show for it.

On both sides of the aid debate, those who shout loudest tend to be the ideologues. The pro-aid camp are too willing to turn a blind eye to the challenges of aid—how sending food hurts farmers, debt cancellation hurts future borrowers, and bypassing governments weakens the political system. Conversely, the anti-aid camp regard the debate in harsh moral terms: if I keep giving you money, you'll never learn to stand on your own two feet.

In this chapter, we'll look at what the data say about making aid work for the poor. What kind of foreign aid works? How much should we worry about corruption, the 'resource curse' and terrorism? I'll also apply one of the classic principles of economics—comparative advantage—to thinking about what kind of foreign aid Australia should deliver. But to kick off, let's bust three common myths about foreign aid: that the only important thing is how much we spend, that we should aim towards zero corruption, and that aid has nothing to do with fighting terrorism.

Myth 1: It's all about the spending. Among the most interesting debates in economics today is the dispute between Jeffrey Sachs and William Easterly over how best to help the world's poor. The discussion is interesting not only because it concerns the most life-and-death question in all of economics, but also because Sachs and Easterly happen to be exceptionally good communicators. Like the long-time Mets–Yankees rivalry, the discussion is the product of a New York state of mind, as they both happen to be at New York universities: Sachs at Columbia University and Easterly at New York University.

At stake is the question of whether development economics requires a 'big push' or piecemeal reform. Sachs, who favours the big push, speaks with the cadences of a great preacher and counts Bono and Angelina Jolie as friends. He argues that the world's least developed countries are caught in a poverty trap, and that success requires a doubling of foreign aid.[2] Sachs claims that aid has achieved spectacular results when directed to economic development (such as the Marshall Plan to rebuild post-war Europe), but lousy results when aimed at political ends (such as the cheques that the United States and the USSR wrote to prop up friendly dictators during the Cold War).

With a grey beard and spectacles, William Easterly is closer to the public image of a dour academic economist. In his writings, Easterly has contended that much foreign aid has been wasted, and that it would be better to focus on taking modest, deliverable steps to make poor people's lives better.[3] Easterly has argued that a 'cartel' of good intentions has meant that aid recipients must meet multiple checklists, covering everything from labour standards to lumber policy, financial information systems to expenditure frameworks. Millions of dollars goes to producing these reports, which often run to hundreds of pages. The focus shifts from saving lives to ticking boxes.

One reason to worry about the effectiveness of aid is that the recipients don't get to vote out bad donor governments. This standard problem of gift-giving will be familiar to anyone who's ever opened a birthday present from a distant relative and thought 'with that much money, I could have bought myself something *so* much nicer'. Unlike voters who judge domestic programs, the recipients of foreign aid cannot punish bad policy at the ballot box. A community may have wanted a road rather than a university, but if the donor government is committed to building universities, they don't have much choice.

To test whether foreign aid works, economists have asked whether countries that receive more aid subsequently experience faster rates of economic growth. In the 1990s, a series of studies reached ambiguous conclusions. A famous research paper in 2000 found that aid did raise growth, so long as the recipient country had good fiscal, monetary and trade policies. Four years later, another study found that these results were fragile, and did not hold up when more years of data were added to the analysis. As though things weren't confusing enough already, another team of researchers concluded that aid had done some good in the world's poorest continent. Even in badly governed Africa, they found, poverty rates would have been significantly higher had the continent received no aid.[4]

So aid can potentially boost growth, but the average effects of aid have been considerably smaller than we'd like. This means that what is done with foreign aid is at least as important as the quantity of aid. More aid creates the potential for reducing poverty—but it's a myth to think that it will happen automatically. (The same principle applies to policy debates about school funding and national defence.)

Myth 2: We can have a zero-corruption aid program. New York City had a parking problem. As home to the United Nations, it plays host to a large number of diplomats. Following a centuries-old tradition, those foreign representatives enjoy diplomatic immunity from prosecution. And in the 1990s, there was little the city could do to prevent diplomats from parking illegally and refusing to pay the parking ticket.

Despite the fact that the same rules applied to all diplomats, two young economists noticed an intriguing puzzle.[5] At the time of their study, there were massive differences in the number of unpaid fines per diplomat across countries. Over a five-year period, the average diplomat from Egypt, Chad and Sudan accumulated an unpaid parking ticket every three weeks. Diplomats from Australia, Sweden and Japan had no outstanding fines whatsoever. The researchers found that diplomats from countries with high corruption ratings were more likely to exploit their diplomatic immunity to accumulate unpaid parking tickets in New York City. True, rich country diplomats could afford to pay their fines, but even holding constant a country's level of development, more corruption back home means more unpaid parking tickets in Manhattan. Cultures of corruption are surprisingly durable.

A cruel fact about the world is that corruption and poverty tend to go together.[6] This presents a dilemma for donors: do we guarantee our dollars never go astray or do we focus on countries and programs where the need is greatest? An aid program that offers technical advice to Korea is less corruption-prone than one that uses local contractors to build pit latrines in Cambodia. But if we care about reducing the number of sick children in the world, building toilets in poor nations is likely to have more effect than providing advice to middle-income countries.

For decades, aid officials have wrestled with the challenge of how to alleviate poverty while minimising losses to corruption. The problem is a bit like a football coach trying to reduce injuries: you don't want the lads to hurt themselves, but a strategy that guarantees no injuries will earn you the wooden spoon.

One of the challenges of development is that poor countries sorely need more construction projects, such as roads and ports. But in developing nations, the construction sector has a reputation for being one of the most corrupt sectors. That's not a coincidence; rather it's a feature of the way construction projects are done. Because each construction project is subtly different, modifications invariably need to be negotiated as the project is built. As development expert Paul Collier has pointed out, the consequence is that 'a large public investment program is dependent upon a sector which is globally corrupt'.[7]

For the world's poor, a new road enables a farmer to access new markets, permits a child to attend secondary school and allows a woman to give birth in hospital. While we work to minimise corruption, we can't forget the benefits of good roads in places such as Indonesia and the Philippines. Thinking like an economist also means counting the cost of graft, and putting it into perspective. One estimate put the losses to fraud at just 3 cents in every $100 that Australia gives in foreign aid. That's considerably smaller than the fraud losses in Australia's domestic social security programs, and probably lower than the fraud losses for businesses operating in Australia. Indeed, the Australian auditor has criticised our aid agency for being too focused on minimising corruption at the expense of resources getting where they are most needed.[8] The problem arises because 'aid fraud' makes the nightly news, while 'aid success' doesn't rate.

Getting aid right is no easy task, particularly with the rise of China as a major donor.[9] There are also plenty of fresh ideas about cutting corruption. For example, the British aid agency was concerned that money intended to pay police officers in Afghanistan had been corruptly skimmed off before it reached them. To combat this type of graft, the aid agency set up a system to pay officers directly, using payment systems linked to their mobile phones.[10] In Indonesia, Australian aid has not only built thousands of schools; it has also created a corruption-control mechanism that has now been adopted by the government to use on all its school-building projects. Like a good football coach, we should do what we can to keep our aid projects off the injury bench—but the war against poverty is the big game.

Myth 3: Aid has nothing to do with fighting terrorism. In a 2013 poll, Muslims in various countries were asked whether suicide bombing against civilian targets is sometimes justified in defence of Islam. Yes, said 62 per cent of Palestinians, 27 per cent of Malaysians, 6 per cent of Indonesians and 3 per cent of Pakistanis.

The rise in terrorism is one of the central facts of our age. In the 1970s, hardly any lives were lost to suicide bombing. In the 2000s, suicide bombers killed more than 10,000 people, including nearly 3000 in the September 11 attacks on New York and Washington DC.[11]

How much does poverty have to do with terrorism? In the past, researchers have pointed out that the typical suicide bomber is better educated than other members of their group.[12] If suicide bombers are well educated, the argument goes, there's not much point building schools to combat terrorism.

The problem with this argument is that it misses the fact that terrorist acts are typically carried out by groups, not lone individuals.[13] It turns out that there is a strong relationship between terrorism and social service provision. It is no accident that the Taliban-run law courts, Hezbollah collects garbage, and Hamas operates health clinics. Social services provide a way of harvesting new recruits and testing their commitment to the leadership. And because social services can be withdrawn at will, providing them gives leverage over the local population, reducing the chance that an informant will leak the latest plan.

Hard as it is to accept, most suicide bombers aren't mentally ill. Interviews with unsuccessful suicide bombers reveal that most truly believe their acts will bring great benefits to their community. To really crush terrorism, we need to show that governments can do a better job of providing social services to help the community that the would-be terrorist cares about. That means using soldiers to protect aid workers who are building new schools, and perhaps even providing security for girls to attend a school in the first few months after it opens.

By helping developing country governments provide services that are currently being delivered by insurgent groups, we can simultaneously help the poor and hurt the terrorists. For example, Egypt's President Nasser undermined the Muslim Brotherhood by nationalising its network of schools and clinics in the 1950s. By directly providing electricity, health care and welfare services, governments improve the outside options for young people.

This is the kind of counter-insurgency approach that one expert has dubbed 'armed social work', because of its ability to unravel the power base of a terrorist organisation.[14] It isn't sexy but it works. As I'll argue below, this is the sort of aid activity at which Australia excels.

What should Australian aid focus on? To answer this question, non-economists might start talking about their favourite programs. For an economist, the starting point needs to be the recognition that Australia is just one of the world's aid donors. That means we need to think in terms of *comparative advantage*.

The principle of comparative advantage is that individuals and nations should specialise in things they do best. Suppose that my wife is a lot better than me at storytelling, and a bit better than me at cooking. Even though she has the absolute advantage in both activities, it makes sense for me to cook dinner and my wife to put our kids to bed. Internationally, the principle of comparative advantage suggests that economies should 'stick to their knitting', rather than trying to produce everything they wish to consume.

Comparative advantage applies to altruism too. Australia accounts for around 2 per cent of world income, so there's a limit on what we can do to solve global poverty. The economics of aid involves confronting these tricky trade-offs. If we have to choose between paying for Jaqueline's HIV treatment, reducing corruption in Papua New Guinea and building schools in Indonesia, what should we pick?

The principle of comparative advantage suggests that Australia should focus on the foreign aid strategies where we do much better than other nations. We need to identify our special skills in reducing poverty, as distinct from offering the programs that any good donor could provide.

As I see it, Australia has three comparative advantages in foreign aid. Our first comparative advantage is that we are unusually well endowed in natural resources. This is particularly important in light of the 'resource curse'—the fact that developing nations that have more natural resources are more likely to be poverty-stricken dictatorships. The 'resource curse' arises because mineral endowments tempt despots into fighting their way into power and filching the wealth. It's difficult for an autocrat to steal incomes from farming, industry or services. But diamonds are a dictator's best friend.

The curse can be seen today in the Democratic Republic of Congo, where conflict over the country's minerals has grown particularly fierce since the mid-1990s, with bands of thugs murdering 5 million people, raping half a million women, and impoverishing a nation. The vast majority of Congo's population would be better off if their country had no natural resources.

Paul Collier pointed out that if we can help developing nations to make better use of their natural resources, the resulting fiscal flows could help societies to transform themselves for the better.[15] In developed nations, oil and mineral assets generally benefit the entire population. In most low-income countries, the opposite is true.

If developing countries can benefit from their minerals, the pay-off could dwarf anything that aid might hope to deliver. On average, the natural resources in a rich nation are worth $114,000 per square kilometre.[16] Or to put it another way, if your home is on a regular-sized block of land, you're sitting on natural resources worth a bit over $100.

For the standard 0.1 hectare (quarter-acre) block, that may sound small, but across a continent, it adds up. Supposing that

Africa's mineral wealth was as big as Europe's, its natural resources would be worth $3.5 trillion. That would be more than 70 times the amount of foreign aid it receives each year. Indeed, $3.5 trillion is probably an underestimate. West Africa has plenty of oil. Central Africa is rich in everything from gold to coltan (used in mobile phones). Southern Africa has bountiful reserves of precious stones.

To help developing nations make better use of their natural resources, a group of entrepreneurs and former politicians have proposed a Natural Resource Charter.[17] The Charter aims to go beyond the ideological slanging match that has characterised natural resource use in developing nations, and offer practical ways in which governments can ensure the people get a better deal. With Australia having enjoyed a mining boom domestically, and around 230 Australian mining companies currently operating in Africa, helping poor countries to better use their natural resources is a clear comparative advantage for Australia.

One proposal in the Charter is to make sure that citizens can follow the money. Mining generates relatively few jobs, so what happens to the royalties is critical. The Charter encourages mining companies to release information about the payments that they make to governments. This makes it harder for corrupt officials and politicians to siphon it off into private bank accounts, and enables citizens to pressure governments into spending the money on much-needed infrastructure, such as hospitals, schools and roads.

Another important change is to ensure that extraction rights are sold by auction. Economists love auctions because they're one of the best ways of making sure an item is sold at fair value. Like a home auction, an auction for rights (such as the right to mine a strip of land) pits rival bidders against one another. When the hammer falls, the bidders have effectively revealed to each other and the seller what they believe the rights are worth. Collier used the example of the UK, which was on the verge of negotiating a £2 billion deal to sell mobile phone spectrum when it was persuaded to try an auction instead. The auction raised over £20 billion. His pitch to developing countries is simple: 'if the British Treasury can get it wrong by a factor of ten, what makes you think you'll do better?'

To help developing countries make the most of their natural resources, governments also need better information. While simple economic theories often assume that people have 'full information', the reality is that poor country governments can sometimes find themselves in a negotiation with a company that's better informed than they are. To get around this, there is a valuable role for aid donors to conduct geological surveys and make them publicly available. When people know what is under the ground, they're more likely to get a fair share of their natural resources.

Australia's second comparative advantage is in dryland farming. As a nation raised on poems about dry river beds, failed crops and dying cattle, it's easy to forget that agriculture in other parts of the world tends to be a rather more stable affair. But this has given Australian farmers more experience in good water management, selection of hardy crops and animals, and management of seed stocks. Wherever possible, we should export our expertise in Australian dryland farming.[18]

Improving agricultural productivity is critical to boosting living standards. The 1960s and 1970s saw a 'green revolution', in which the combination of hybrid seeds, manufactured fertilisers, pesticides and herbicides massively raised agricultural output. By one estimate, the green revolution saved a billion people from starvation. Yet today, African farms produce less than half as much food per hectare as the global average, and Africa imports more food than it exports. Part of the reason is that Africans tend to use inferior seeds, less fertiliser and fewer machines. For example, the continent has only one tractor per 868 hectares, compared with one tractor per 56 hectares globally. One success story has been Malawi, which has recently doubled agricultural output through the combination of modern seeds and fertilisers. We should consider whether elements of that model can be extended to other African nations, perhaps through innovative financing. Helping farmers also has a critical gender dimension, since 70 per cent of developing country farmers are women.[19]

Another implication of dryland farming is price volatility. Some climate models predict increased rainfall volatility in Africa's Sahel, a region containing Chad and Niger, where average incomes are less than a dollar a day.[20] Closer to home, Pacific island nations are likely to lose fresh water supplies and fertile land to sea-water inundations. Some have suggested that aid agencies should work with developing country governments to provide drought insurance to rural households.[21] Australia's drought assistance schemes have their critics, but given Australia's expertise in designing such schemes for our own farmers, this is a natural area for our aid workers to be involved in.

Australia can also help in international trade negotiations. As a major exporter of agricultural products, we set up the Cairns Group of agricultural free-trading nations in 1986. Today, Australia has a strong interest in arguing against policies that harm farmers in developing countries as well as in our own. If the United States was to abolish its ethanol subsidies and the European Union was to adopt a more science-based approach to genetically modified foodstuffs, agriculture in developing countries would be more viable.

Our third comparative advantage is operating in post-conflict environments. From our experience in East Timor and the Solomon Islands, Australia has acquired valuable experience in restoring normality to strife-torn regions. Of the top five recipients of Australian foreign aid, four are countries that are often described as 'fragile states'.[22]

Getting intervention right in post-conflict environments involves some delicate balancing acts. One of my favourite stories is told by journalist Robert Guest:[23]

Somalia has no government, unless you count a 'transitional'
one that controls a few streets in the capital, Mogadishu, and

a short stretch of coastline. The rest of the country is divided into warring fiefdoms. Warlords extract protection money from anyone who has money to extract. Clans, sub-clans, and sub-sub-clans pursue bloody vendettas against each other, often fighting over grudges that pre-date the colonial period. Few children learn to read, but practically all self-respecting young men carry submachine-guns.

I was at one of the country's countless road blocks, on a sandy road outside Baidoa, a southern town of shell-blasted stone walls and sandy streets. The local warlord's men were waving their Kalashnikovs at approaching trucks, forcing them to stop. Many of the trucks carried passengers perched atop the cargoes of logs or oil drums. The men with guns then ordered all the children under five to dismount and herded them into the shade of a nearby tree. There, they handed them over to strangers with clipboards, who squeezed open their mouths and fed each one a single drop of polio vaccine.

Robert Guest was describing vaccination work carried out by the World Health Organization, which decided that working with local warlords to distribute polio vaccine was the lesser of two evils.

Aid to fragile states requires considerable political nous. In 2003, when the Solomon Islands was being torn apart by civil war, the country's prime minister asked Australian forces to help avoid a meltdown. Within weeks, an Australian force of 2250 military and police had successfully stabilised the situation—persuading the nastiest gang leaders to surrender, collecting thousands of weapons but not antagonising the local population.[24] At the main Australian base (located outside Honiara), military personnel had more than enough training and firepower to take on the toughest thugs in town, yet the police officers visible to most Solomon Islanders were unarmed.

The challenge in stabilising a fragile state is to provide enough military might to protect the local population, but not to use so much force that you galvanise people into joining the opposition. In recent decades, the world has seen examples of efforts that have been too soft and too harsh. In Srebrenica in 1995, a force of Dutch peace-keepers failed to fire on advancing Serb soldiers, leading to the Srebrenica Massacre of more than 8000 men and boys—Europe's worst post-war atrocity. In 2003, the United States–led occupation of Iraq was marred by a series of blunders—often because troops used more force than necessary, and alienated local Iraqis. By contrast, the Australian-led stabilisation missions in East Timor in 1999 and in the Solomons four years later managed to achieve their goals with virtually no harm to civilians or Australian forces.

Every stabilisation operation is different, so it's hard to separate the effectiveness of an intervention from the challenges it faces. But I do have a sense that Australia's style of military and policing—firmer than the Europeans, but more sensitive than the Americans—is suited to the fact that the rise of terrorism is blurring the lines between military, policing and aid operations. For example, Australia's training role in Afghanistan's Uruzgan province was done in an environment where literacy rates were 8 per cent for men and 1 per cent for women. Better education is one of our most powerful tools for economic development, better governance, and stopping extremism. And although Australia's record on gender equality isn't perfect, our aid program is increasingly looking for opportunities to work with women leaders in developing nations.

On Boxing Day 2004, a massive undersea earthquake occurred off the coast of Indonesia. With a magnitude of 9.2 on the Richter scale, it was the third-largest quake ever recorded. As the sea floor buckled, waves up to 30 metres high raced towards the coast. As a child, I lived for two years in the Indonesian province of Aceh, just 160 kilometres from the epicentre of the quake. Acehnese friends told my parents about how the tsunami had plucked infants from their parents' arms. In total, 170,000 Indonesians were killed.

In the Sri Lankan town of Ambalangoda, a train was unloading goods when local authorities phoned the stationmaster to warn him not to let it continue along a coastal stretch of track. But the stationmaster was too busy to take the call, and the train left the station. Without a mobile phone, there was no way to warn the driver. At a coastal village, the tsunami threw the train off the tracks like a child's toy. Almost all of the passengers were killed.[25]

With 230,000 victims worldwide, the Boxing Day Tsunami was one of the deadliest natural disasters in world history. With little else to occupy the world media during January 2005, the tsunami received near-blanket coverage over subsequent weeks. In total, the Australian government donated $1.4 billion, and the public gave another $280 million. Globally, donations came to around US$14 billion.

At the time, many commentators attributed this to intrinsic generosity. But might it also have had to do with the timing of the tsunami? Or to put the question another way: if the disaster had been on page 10 rather than the front page, would donors have been as generous?

A pair of economics studies suggest that the answer is probably no. In one Australian analysis, researchers looked at several overseas disasters, and compared the number of newspaper articles with the amount of public donations (by the Australian government) and private donations (by individuals to World Vision).[26] They found that the relationship was strong and positive. More articles in the press meant significantly more private and public disaster assistance.

But what if disasters receive more news coverage because they're severe, or because the victims are needier? How can we be sure that donors are giving because there are more stories in the press, rather than simply because the disaster is bigger?

To get at the true causal effect of the press, we need media coverage to vary for some reason unrelated to the crisis itself.

So a pair of Swedish economists came up with a novel solution.[27] Rather than start with disasters, they began by looking at domestic events that might distract people's attention from global disasters. When a nation is preoccupied with a local story, does it become less generous? Focusing on 30 years of US disaster assistance, the study analyses what happens when an overseas famine, volcano or flood occurs at the same time as an event of local interest such as the Olympics, the O.J. Simpson trial, or an American school shooting.

It turns out that when the US media is preoccupied with another story, it is less likely to pay attention to the international crisis. In turn, this has a direct effect on US government donations. To have the same chance of receiving US assistance, a disaster that coincides with the Olympics needs to have three times as many casualties as a disaster occurring on a regular news day.

Coverage of international disasters also seems to skew aid in other ways. In both Australia and the United States, visually dramatic events such as volcanoes and floods receive significantly more media than famines and civil wars. For every person killed in a volcano disaster, 40,000 people must die in a drought to receive as much media coverage. Access matters too. For an African disaster to receive as much media coverage as an Eastern European disaster, 40 times as many people must die.

These studies have profound implications for slow-moving African crises, such as the humanitarian crisis in Darfur. With fewer images to put on the television screen and the front page, Darfur rarely rates a mention outside the foreign affairs pages of serious newspapers. As a result, Sudan's evacuees probably receive a smaller share of international assistance than would people displaced by a volcano in Southeast Asia.

Sometimes the neediest causes are not the most newsworthy. Several months after the Boxing Day tsunami, a famine in Niger killed around 360,000 people. This was a higher death toll than in the tsunami. But the Niger famine received minimal media coverage, and attracted less than 1 per cent of the aid that went to tsunami-affected countries.

Geo-politics affects aid flows too. Earlier, I mentioned Jeffrey Sachs' observation that the Cold War saw aid used to buy support in the power games between the United States and the Soviet Union. Even now, aid is used to influence elections. In the year when a developing country government is up for election, it tends to get more aid from donors who share its political views. When a developing nation wins one of the temporary seats on the United Nations Security Council, the amount of foreign aid it gets from the United States goes up by more than 50 per cent.[28]

The coincidence of geopolitics and the luck of the press can prevent aid going where it's most needed. In our daily lives, all of us find ourselves tempted to let urgent things crowd out important ones. Who of us hasn't skipped a gym visit to watch a favourite television program, checked email when we should be working on an important report, or picked up leaves in the garden because it's easier than fixing the broken tile on the roof? But in the area of foreign aid, lives are at stake, so getting it right really matters.

People like Jaqueline Lima may live a long way away, but we can still help them to live longer and healthier lives. In addition, as development economics teaches us, aid can have unexpected effects: for example, better social services mean fewer terrorists. And in a world where Australia can't end all the poverty around us, we might consider using the economic principle of comparative advantage to guide us: helping countries get the most from their mineral wealth, assisting dryland farming and stabilising fragile states.

Smashing the crystal ball

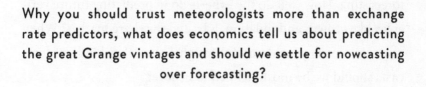

Why you should trust meteorologists more than exchange rate predictors, what does economics tell us about predicting the great Grange vintages and should we settle for nowcasting over forecasting?

In April 2010, economist Steve Keen set out on a 235-kilometre trek from Parliament House in Canberra to the top of Mount Kosciuszko. He was wearing a T-shirt bearing the words 'I was hopelessly wrong on house prices! Ask me how.' In a November 2008 debate with Macquarie Group economist Rory Robertson, Keen had forecast that house prices would fall by at least 20 per cent. In fact, 2009 saw Australian house prices rise by more than 10 per cent.[1]

As the saying goes, it's difficult to make predictions, especially about the future.[2] Considering the possibility of train travel that exceeded 15 kilometres an hour, an 1825 writer opined: 'What can be more palpably absurd and ridiculous than the prospect held out of locomotives travelling twice as fast as stage-coaches!'

In 1912, radio pioneer Guglielmo Marconi stated: 'The coming of the wireless era will make war impossible.' Two years later, World War I began. In 2007, Microsoft CEO Steve Ballmer said, 'There's no chance that the iPhone is going to get any significant market share.'[3]

'The only function of economic forecasting', said Harvard economist John Kenneth Galbraith, 'is to make astrology look respectable.' In this chapter, I'll assess the Australian evidence on forecasting. How well do the experts do in predicting future variables like growth and inflation, jobs and the share market? When can economists provide useful insights and what kinds of forecasts should we be most inclined to believe?

Forecasts matter. We rely on information from meteorologists to decide whether to ride a bike to work or take the train. Governments depend on threat predictions in deciding how to spend their military budget and on demographic forecasts in deciding where to build the next hospital. If you're signing up for a three-year bachelor degree, chances are you want to choose something that will be in demand from employers by the time you graduate. Knowing how much you can trust predictions is a question that affects the lives of each of us.

Let's start with forecasts of the economy. Knowing what's going to happen to growth next year is absolutely vital if you're running a business. Should you hire more staff, buy a new vehicle and expand the marketing budget? Or is it better to accumulate a bit of spare cash on the balance sheet? Make the right call and you can turn a small business into a big one. Make the wrong call and you'll be talking with the liquidators.

In a quest to predict the cycle of boom and bust, a variety of innovative theories have emerged. Some are practical. The 'cardboard box index' is based on the idea that three-quarters of consumer goods are shipped in boxes. Because companies have to buy the boxes wholesale before they ship the product, the theory suggests that boxes are a good leading indicator for surges or slumps in the economy. Similarly, the 'men's underwear index' suggests that because your underwear is seen by few people, it might be one of the first things that people start to cut back on when the economy turns bad. One commentator compares men deferring underwear purchases in tough times to the way that others might drive their car an extra 10,000 kilometres between services.[4]

Other theories are more psychological. The 'hemline index' proposes that skirt lengths rise in good times and fall in bad times. Advocates of this theory point out that skirts were shorter in the roaring 1920s than in the hard times of the 1930s and that the miniskirt emerged in the boom times of the 1960s. The 'music index' suggests that in hard times we are more likely to listen to songs that are slower, more comforting and more romantic. And the 'centrefold index' suggests that in tough economic conditions, magazine models tend to be taller, older and have larger waists.[5]

Alas, when researchers have looked carefully into these theories, there's little evidence they can tell us anything about the future (indeed, hemlines appears to track economic conditions three years *earlier*). But what happens when we move from folk wisdom to business commentators? Can business pundits predict the future?

About every six months since 1979, the *Age* newspaper has been asking a group of prominent commentators to estimate economic growth in the future. Alas, they haven't exactly covered themselves in glory. In December 1988, the *Age* asked 42 commentators to estimate how much the economy would grow in calendar year 1989. Their answers ranged from 0.8 per cent to 3.75 per cent. In fact, the economy grew 4.6 per cent that year.

Less than two years later, in July 1990, the *Age* asked 38 commentators—many of them the same people who had failed to predict that the economy would grow at 4.6 per cent—to estimate the growth rate for the fiscal year 1990–91. Their answers ranged from 0.5 per cent to 2.8 per cent. Ultimately, the economy shrank by 0.8 per cent, a slump Treasurer Paul Keating described as 'the recession we had to have'. As a nation, it's possible that we might have been able to take quicker action to soften the hard landing of the 1990s recession if only forecasters had seen it coming.

In the space of two years, the nation's business forecasters had been surprised twice. None had predicted how fast the economy would grow in 1989. None predicted that the economy would shrink in 1990–91. In 1998–99, the economy grew faster than all 28 *Age* commentators had predicted. In 2007, the *Age* summed up its commentators' forecasts for the following year as 'The good times are rolling'. Then the global financial crisis hit, and Australia grew more slowly than all 21 commentators had predicted.[6]

To systematically assess the accuracy of a prediction, we need something to compare it against. In the case of growth, economists typically use as a benchmark the naive assumption that next year's growth rate will be the same as this year's growth rate. Think of this as the pet parrot approach, in which you teach your parrot to say the current growth rate. Any time someone asks it to forecast next year's economy, it will dutifully squawk this year's number.

Do business forecasters beat the parrot? Yes, but not by much. When it came to forecasting growth, the typical forecaster was off by 0.9 percentage points, while the parrot would have been wrong by 1.1 percentage points.[7] In other words, business commentators polled by the *Age* were only about one-fifth better than a pet parrot—and that's what you get when you average their forecasts (effectively allowing the pessimists and optimists to cancel one another out). Take any single commentator, and the chance that he or she will beat the parrot is slim indeed.

To their credit, both the Reserve Bank and Treasury have recently published estimates of their own forecasts. Assessing the predictive power of their economic forecasts over nearly two decades, the Reserve Bank concluded that its forecasts of future unemployment and future growth were generally *less* accurate than the naive estimate.[8] Only on inflation was the Reserve Bank able to trounce the parrot.

The story from Treasury is disappointingly similar. A major review of Treasury forecasts over twenty years found that they beat the parrot in forecasting real growth but not in forecasting inflation.[9]

As David Gruen, a senior macroeconomist in Treasury, put it: 'economic forecasters aren't stupid; what we are trying to do is hard!'[10] Droughts, the rise of China and the ubiquitous use of smart phones are transforming whole sectors of the Australian economy. Even births and deaths can be hard to forecast. In 2002, Treasury unveiled its first *Intergenerational Report*—designed to focus the minds of Australians on long-term challenges. It predicted that by 2010 our population growth rate would fall below 1 per cent. But by the time 2010 came around, Australian women were having more babies and the nation was taking in more immigrants, pushing our population growth rate above 2 per cent. In the 2002 *Intergenerational Report*, Treasury forecast that by the 2040s, Australia's population would be 26 million. In its 2010 *Intergenerational Report*, they had updated that to 35 million.[11] What are nine million Aussies between friends?

Other forecasters specialise in estimating what will happen to the labour market, advising governments which industries to invest in, and individuals which careers to follow. Alas, employment forecasters too struggle to beat the parrot. Figure 4 shows the relationship between forecasts published in 1995 for the labour market and the actual employment results over the ensuing decade.[12] The report was trying to answer a simple

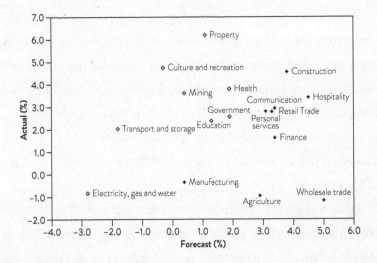

Figure 4: Comparing employment forecasts with actual results

question: which of the seventeen industries—shown as dots in Figure 4—would exhibit the strongest employment growth?

If the forecasters had done their job perfectly, the points on the scatterplot should line up precisely in a diagonal line. This would mean that an industry forecast to shrink by 1 per cent actually shrank by 1 per cent, and an industry forecast to grow by 4 per cent actually grew by 4 per cent. But in fact the forecasts are scattered across the chart. Industries that grew more slowly than predicted have solid markers, and those that grew faster than expected have hollow markers. For example, culture and recreation was projected to shrink, and ended up growing by 5 per cent. Wholesale trade was projected to grow by 5 per cent and ended up shrinking.

Another error was in forecasting mining employment, which was projected to stay stable and ended up growing by nearly 4 per cent. This reflected the common beliefs of the era (a 1999 report projected that future mining employment would *shrink*). Indeed, even polymath Barry Jones said in 2001: 'we are perceived as having an economy based on the exploitation of raw materials, that is, an Old Economy'. By the end of the decade, mining's share of the economy had doubled.[13]

Forecasts of the labour market are inaccurate for the same reason as predictions about growth and inflation are problematic: the economy is a complex system, subject to sudden shocks. Analysing forecasts of the US labour market, Harvard's Richard Freeman explained why the projections turn out so badly: jobs are more likely to be affected by disruptive changes such as technology and trade than slow-moving forces such as demography.[14] He gave the example of computer programmers, where demand grew faster than forecasters expected in the late 1990s dot-com boom, then slower than anticipated in the early 2000s after the dot-com bust. Indeed, the only really reliable labour market forecasts are for skills: given that the unemployment rate is lowest for highly educated workers, it's a safe bet that the labour market in the future will continue to demand more educated employees.

Another set of forecasters are those who claim to be able to predict the share market. A fundamental lesson from economics is that, in an efficient market, share prices incorporate all publicly available information about the firm. Consequently, short-run changes in share prices cannot be predicted. As Burton Malkiel put it in his 1973 classic, *A Random Walk Down Wall Street*, this means that a portfolio chosen by 'a blindfolded monkey throwing darts at a newspaper's financial pages . . . would do just as well as one carefully selected by the experts'.[15]

A clear implication of Malkiel's study is that investors cannot make money from obvious information. For example, the rise in Australia's birthrate has boosted consumer demand for baby toys. But any consequent increase in profitability in toy-making companies has already been factored into their share prices. The only way to be sure you're going to beat the market is if you know a secret about the company (such as the fact that the CEO is about to resign). But if you got that information because you work at the company, it's illegal for you to trade on it.

Because share markets are reasonably efficient at incorporating public information, it's hard even for well-informed people to outperform the market. An analysis of actively traded Australian share funds found that they typically beat the market by about half a percentage point. Alas, because the typical fund charged a management fee of about 1 per cent, the typical share fund underperforms the market by about half a percentage point. Only one-fifth of actively traded funds beat the market.[16] Predicting share prices turns out to be pretty hard.

But if there's any set of forecasters who inadvertently make all the others look good, it's exchange rate forecasters. Every day, billions of dollars are traded on the foreign exchange market. Even a tiny edge in the forecasting game could make you an instant fortune. Alas, there's little evidence to suggest that anyone can do a good job of anticipating future exchange rates. In 2000, Chief Scientist Robin Batterham suggested that the Australian dollar could fall from 50 US cents to 30 US cents within a decade.[17] Over the subsequent ten years, the value of the Australian dollar tripled.

Forecasts from large banks are just as flawed. In 2009, major banks ANZ and Westpac predicted that the dollar would fall from 63 cents to 55 cents. Instead, it rose to 92 cents. In 2011, asset manager Savvas Savouri predicted that the Australian dollar would hit $1.70 in 2014.[18] At the time of writing, his prediction isn't looking good. As Melbourne Business School's Mark Crosby points out, 'one of the most robust empirical results in macroeconomics is the idea that the nominal exchange rate is a random walk'. In other words, the exchange rate is equally likely to rise or fall.

An intuitive way to think about this is to suppose you knew for sure that the Australian dollar would be worth less in a year. In that case, you'd convert all your money into US dollars today, convert it back in a year's time, and make a tidy profit. The trouble is, if *everyone* knows that the dollar will fall in a year's time, then everyone would do this. Result: the dollar falls today. As Crosby warns, 'Private forecasting models that assume predictable movements in the exchange rate are not defensible.' The best guess of tomorrow's exchange rate is today's exchange rate. The same holds true of any variable that follows a random walk: forecasting it makes as little sense as forecasting whether a coin will come up heads or tails.

In his book on forecasting, statistics boffin Nate Silver argued that one of the few professions with a strong track record of forecast accuracy is weather forecasting. On average, when the Bureau of Meteorology says that there is a 20 per cent chance of rain, it does in fact rain one day out of five. Weather forecasters are now better at forecasting three days in advance than they were at forecasting one day in advance in the early 1980s.[19] Part of the reason for this is that we have a reasonably good model of how weather works, and that model becomes better when we have more sensors and faster computers. Last year, I helped open Australia's fastest supercomputer on the Australian National University's campus. The machine is bigger than a house. If you're standing between the banks of microprocessors when they start working, it's hotter than a midsummer day. One of the main jobs the ANU supercomputer will do is to improve the accuracy of weather forecasts.

So, overall, forecasters tend to do badly. But listen to the news for a few days and you're likely to hear a plethora of forecasts. Why do we keep giving airtime to bad forecasters? The answer lies in the economics of demand and supply. As humans, we have a strong desire to know how the future will turn out—a demand for high-quality forecasts. But there aren't many high-quality forecasts around, so low-quality forecasts step in to fill the void. We're yearning for Dr Who's Tardis, but we end up talking to palm readers and tarot card shysters instead. When these forecasters fail—as they so often do—they're ready with excuses such as 'I was almost right', 'I would have been right if something fluky didn't occur', or 'I could still be right if we wait long enough'.[20]

So how can we get a better crystal ball? One solution is to swap experts for prediction markets, which have proven more accurate in forecasting the future. Such markets aggregate information from a large number of individuals, weighting it in proportion to each person's degree of certainty about the outcome. Ask experts what they think will happen and you'll discover that talk can be pretty cheap. Ask those same experts how much money they'd wager that the predicted event will come to pass and you'll find out how confident they really are.

Over the past decade, a wealth of evidence has accumulated on the power of prediction markets. In the words of George Mason University's Robin Hanson: 'in every known head-to-head field comparison between speculative markets and other social institutions that forecast, the markets have been no less, and usually more, accurate . . . horse race markets beat horse race experts, Oscar markets beat columnist forecasts, gas demand markets beat gas demand experts'.[21] And many firms—including General Electric, Google, Hewlett Packard, Nokia and Pfizer—have established internal prediction markets to shape their decision-making.

An analysis of futures markets in economic indicators such as employment and retail sales found that these 'macroeconomic derivatives' performed at least as well as the average from a panel of professional forecasters. Another study looked at 'influenza prediction markets', and found that the market was able to accurately forecast flu activity up to one month in advance.[22]

The same thing holds in sport. To test the efficiency of sports betting markets, I joined in my office AFL tipping competition, following a simple strategy: look at the betting markets, and back the favourite. At the end of the season, this strategy had correctly predicted the results of 77 per cent of games.[23] I didn't win the tipping competition, but managed to beat six-sevenths of my co-workers. Had I been offering tips for a major newspaper, it's likely that I would have outperformed most of the other 'experts' on the panel.[24] On reflection, it's hardly a surprise that betting markets trounce expert tipsters. If you had information that would allow you to win tens of thousands of dollars every week, would you share it with the paper? Another study has shown tennis betting markets to be good real-time predictors of match outcomes, quickly responding to events such as service breaks.[25]

One way of thinking about prediction markets is that they weight everyone's predictions by how confident they are in the outcome. Are you likely to bet on macroeconomic indicators tonight? I'm guessing not, probably because you don't think you have special insights. But those who made the largest punts are those who are most confident they know something about the markets. Prediction markets are not perfect—just better than the alternatives.[26] Trading volumes are generally thick enough to provide good estimates, and arbitrage opportunities are rare. Market manipulation is difficult and prices generally revert to their true value as smart money happily soaks up ideological wagers. Structural details—such as whether the markets are run as betting markets or futures exchanges—do not seem to matter much.

Prediction markets are an example of a better forecasting tool that we should rely upon more often. But sometimes we're dealing with things that simply can't be reliably forecast. Share prices are one such example. We know on average that shares are a good investment: indeed, advisers typically suggest that a person in their twenties or thirties should have more than half of their investments in shares. But picking which stocks will rise fastest turns out to be extremely difficult—even for the experts—so the best approach is not to pay people too much to manage your money. Instead, you're more likely to benefit from putting your money in an 'index fund', which simply tracks the average of the share market. If the whole share market rises 10 per cent, your index fund goes up 10 per cent, less a very small management fee. Indeed, the main difference between active funds and index funds isn't the returns before fees, it's the fact that active funds charge a fat fee, and index funds charge a slim one.

The other way to avoid fees is to trade less often. In most share markets around the world, it turns out that the typical 'buy and hold' return is higher than the 'dollar-weighted' return. From the mid-1970s to the mid-2000s, the typical stock on the Australian market earned a return of 12.3 per cent per year.[27] But the typical investment dollar earned an annual return of 11.7 per cent. The problem is that investors tend to buy and sell at the wrong times, over-investing in stocks just before they peak. Investors think that they are forecasting the next big thing, when in fact they're jumping from fad to fad, and paying brokerage fees along the way.

The same holds for the market as a whole. When the global financial crisis caused share market prices to fall, one in twenty Australian superannuation investors switched their investment choices, with many switching from shares to cash. As University of Western Australia finance professor Paul Gerrans noted, this 'meant a double hit from the declines experienced until that point, without the compensation of the subsequent market rebound'.[28] Rather than think that they could forecast the future, most would have been better gritting their teeth and staying put. In fact, the problem isn't all that different from the one we often face at the supermarket. If you've waited for a while in one checkout line, it's rarely a good idea to switch.

Another modest response to the generally dismal performance of forecasters has been to put more effort into understanding what is happening today. Google's 'nowcasting' project aims to provide real-time indicators of what is happening in the economy and society.

If that sounds unambitious, it's worth realising how much of a lag is built into our current statistics. For influenza numbers, it's two weeks. For unemployment, it's six weeks. For inflation, it's eight weeks. And growth statistics are released with a 12-week lag.[29] In rough economic times, that makes policy like driving a car down a winding road while watching out the rear-vision mirror.

By contrast, Google flu trends turn out to provide early warning of a sudden spike in flu cases. Australian consumer confidence fits closely the number of Google searches for new vehicles (and, surprisingly, crime). Researchers at the Bank of England found that UK house prices track searches for 'estate agents'.[30] Note that in each case, we're 'nowcasting' rather than 'futurecasting', but it's still better than looking out the rear window.

In the case of unemployment, searches for 'welfare' and 'unemployment' spiked in the United States in mid-2008, just as the national jobless rate passed 5 per cent. Before the welfare data and labour force surveys had been compiled, search data could have indicated to economic policymakers that storm clouds were gathering. And given the well-known lags in fiscal policy, search data is worth using any time we're worried about a future downturn.

A cute feature of using search data to look at joblessness is that it also points to distinct patterns of search terms among the unemployed—many of whom are young men. Google chief economist Hal Varian has found that the first set of terms to spike is labour-market related ('jobs classifieds', 'unemployment benefits'). The second phase sees an increase in searches for new technologies ('iPod apps', 'free ringtone'). The third stage of unemployment searches is for low-cost entertainment ('guitar scales beginner', 'home workout routines'). The fourth stage of unemployment searches is for adult content ('adult video', 'porn tube').[31]

Rivalling Elisabeth Kübler-Ross's 'five stages of grief', Google's 'four stages of unemployment' is a touching story about how the US recession has affected everyday life. The stages of unemployment searches are as much a part of life as the fact that an increased search volume for 'vodka' is followed by a spike in searches for 'hangover cure'. They may not allow us to forecast the future but they do tell us a lot about today. Indeed, just as credit card firms rely on real-time data to run their businesses, so too Australian universities might benefit from a heads-up when search volumes suddenly shift from 'accounting ATAR' to 'engineering ATAR'.

Economics doesn't just teach us to be wary of pundits bearing forecasts—it's also able to use new data to better understand the world around us. And just as 'nowcasting' has led the Google geeks into areas like predicting disease outbreaks, wine economists have found that they can use data to predict the quality of an 'unborn' wine.

Wait, I hear you say. Wine economists? Yes, you read that right. In the 1990s, Princeton University economist Orley Ashenfelter caused a ruckus in the wine world when he showed that the sale prices of Bordeaux wines were strongly related to the weather patterns during the growing season.[32] Top wines may take 20 to 50 years to reach their peak, so swish-and-spit wine buffs devote considerable energy to determining whether a newly released wine will go on to be a great vintage. Kym Anderson, a wine economist at the University of Adelaide, told the story:

When Orley first started doing this work, the wine critics were just incensed. He said the 1989 and 1990 Bordeaux would be outstanding, and everybody said 'that's just ridiculous', because it didn't match with what critics were saying from the tastings. And of course it turned out they were great years. But now, if you read wine critics, the good ones almost always include information about the weather. So they have accepted that this is reality—you can tell not just from your taste buds, but also from the weather. Or if you're in doubt, then maybe look at the weather and forget about your taste buds![33]

Intrigued by the possibility of forecasting future wines, I set about updating past work of Ashenfelter and Anderson, focusing on predicting the quality of Australia's most famous wine: Penfolds Grange Hermitage.[34] Not only is Grange famous worldwide, it also has the advantage of being blended from grapes at vineyards across South Australia.[35] A good Grange year also tends to be a good year for Adelaide shiraz wines in general.

To test the relationship, I obtained weather data from the Bureau of Meteorology and Grange auction data from Kym Anderson.[36] I then set about seeing how well the weather can explain wine prices, using a technique known as multiple regression. The short answer is 'surprisingly well'. On average, the weather can explain about three-quarters of the variation in Grange auction prices. To put this into perspective, most attempts to explain prices only succeed in accounting for a small portion of the differences. As

I noted in Chapter 4, if I know the age, education and gender of a group of people, I'll only be able to explain about one-tenth of the differences between what they earn each hour. So to be able to account for three-quarters of the variation means that weather matters a great deal for wine prices.

The model suggests that Granges are better when there is less rain at the start of harvest season (January and February), when the temperature during the growing season (October to March) is as close as possible to 20.0 degrees Celsius, and when there is less variation in temperature (that is, the minimum and maximum temperatures are closer together).[37] If you had nothing but the weather reports, you would have predicted that the 1971 vintage (which wine buffs often call 'the greatest of the Granges') would be excellent, and that the 1972 vintage would be very ordinary (largely due to heavy rains at the start of the harvest season). The model also suggests that climate change will reduce the quality of future Granges (unless Penfolds draws more heavily on grapes grown in cooler locations).

But not only can I use this technique to explain past wine auction prices: because weather data are available up to the day, I can also use it to project which will be the best future Granges. And because wines like Grange take at least twenty years to mature, this allows me to forecast the future. In Table 7, I show how the weather model ranks the last twenty years' worth of Grange vintages, and compare my forecasts with a set of expert assessments from Langton's, a major wine auctioneer.[38]

Table 7: Using weather data to predict Grange vintages

Vintage	Weather model rank (out of 10)	Expert rank (out of 10)
1993	10	6
1994	8	9
1995	7	6
1996	7	10
1997	8	6
1998	9	10
1999	10	9
2000	9	7
2001	2	9
2002	6	10
2003	2	6
2004	6	10
2005	10	8
2006	4	9
2007	2	7
2008	2	8
2009	9	NR
2010	1	10
2011	9	7
2012	5	NR
2013	4	NR

NR = not rated by Langton's

Comparing the assessments, the first difference you notice is that my assessments use the full 1 to 10 scale, while the experts rate from 6 to 10. This isn't to say that I think a Grange rated 1/10 would be worse than your average bottle of cheap wine: merely that the weather model predicts it will be in the worst tenth of all the Grange vintages in the past 60 years.

While the weather model has something in common with the experts during the 1990s, the big divergence comes for recent years.[39] When it was released in 2013 (at a retail price of $785), the 2008 vintage was rated pretty highly by the experts. Indeed, Robert Parker's *Wine Advocate* gave it a perfect 100 points. But it was grown in a season where the temperature averaged 21 degrees (1 degree above the optimum), and where the temperatures fluctuated a lot. The weather model rates the 2008 as 2/10.

We differ even more over the unreleased vintages. Langton's described the 2010 as a 'classically structured and beautifully proportioned Grange'.[40] My statistical model just sees that the growing season was the hottest in 60 years, averaging 21.5 degrees, with big temperature swings from daytime to night-time. Without having consumed a sip of the 2010 vintage, I think it will be one of the least impressive Granges ever produced. The weather model rates it 1/10. In a couple of decades' time, the 2010 should be coming into its prime, and we'll know whether my weather model outperforms the quaffers.

In 2001, while working at a think-tank in Washington, DC, I co-authored a report on the 'digital divide' in the United States. After looking at the trend in computer ownership and internet penetration rates, we concluded that by 2005, 90 per cent of US households would have a computer in the home and be connected to the internet. It was a bold prediction, and turned out to be hopelessly wrong. Even now, fewer than 80 per cent of US households have computers and an internet connection.[41] Indeed, given the rise in smart phones, it now seems possible that the 90 per cent target might never be met. If Rory Robertson had been around to throw down a bet in 2001, I might have found myself walking to Mount Kosciuszko in a T-shirt that said: 'I was hopelessly wrong on the digital divide! Ask me how.'

Predicting the future is hard—really hard. Hemlines and song rhythms don't predict economic growth, but then again, neither do the expert forecasters do a great job. Among a few dozen of the nation's top business commentators, not one picked the 1991 recession or the 2008 downturn. Share prices, birthrates and jobs are tough to predict, and exchange rates are near impossible. In each case, that's because the big drivers of social change are disruptive technologies and sudden shifts in society. When I made my failed forecast about US computer ownership, I was looking at past computer adoption rates, and comparing them with adoption rates for televisions and VCRs. I was utterly blindsided by the rise of smart phones.

Not all forecasts are hopeless. Some predictors—such as weather forecasters—are pretty accurate (perhaps because they typically look days rather than years ahead). Weather reports have even managed to forecast a good Grange. In other areas, we can rely on tools such as prediction markets (which do a little better). Sometimes, we need to recognise that it's better to stop paying unsuccessful experts (such as active money managers) or to focus on getting a handle on what's happening today (as with Google's nowcasting project).

As good economists know, forecasting is an area where there is more demand for quality forecasts than supply of decent forecasters. Philip Tetlock, who has studied expert forecasters, described the characteristic of a bad predictor in one word: 'dogmatism'. By contrast, he says, good forecasters are able to engage in constructive self-criticism. Good forecasters aren't dumbfounded by the question 'what would it take to convince you you're wrong?'[42]

To again use the famous metaphor of Oxford philosopher Isaiah Berlin, good forecasters are less likely to be hedgehogs (who know one big thing) and more likely to be foxes (who know many things).[43] Sometimes it's hopeless to forecast the future (exchange rate forecasters, I'm looking at you). But in many cases a clever fox can help to build a better crystal ball.

Playing the blue guitar

Why we buy black cars on cloudy days, how a clean desk memo sunk a CEO and what is the deadweight cost of Christmas?

On the goldfields of Ballarat in the 1850s, there were three men for every woman. Historian Clare Wright described how this generated a situation in which 'women could pluck husbands like so many wild flowers'. Diggers would come down to the dock to meet ships, hoping to induce women to marry them. One girl wrote home to her sisters in England: 'I had an offer a few days after landing from a gold-digger, with £600–£700. Since that I have had another from a bushman, with £600 . . . I shall have a handsome house and garden and all I wish.'[1]

The skewed gender ratio didn't just allow women to marry richer men—it also affected their status within the marriage. One who had emigrated advised other women to follow her example: 'Do so by all means, the worst risk you run is that of getting married and finding yourself treated with twenty times the respect and consideration you may meet in England.'[2] In economic terms, women on the goldfields were scarce. Men were plentiful. The marriage market responded by moving to a new equilibrium, which was more favourable to women and less so for men.

In a sense, you can think of this book as being inspired by *The Art of Fugue*. Bach's masterwork starts with a simple 12-note theme in D minor. He then produces 18 more fugues by variously inverting the theme, halving note lengths, doubling note lengths, playing it like a round, and even weaving various versions of the theme across itself. That's what I've aimed to do here—weave the themes of economics through a variety of different situations. Indeed, it's how I tried to teach introductory economics to students at the Australian National University—aiming to ensure that people immersed themselves in the big ideas, and could apply them to a host of circumstances.[3]

Once you start thinking like an economist, you begin seeing the world differently. Take trade-offs, for example. Because economists think about trade-offs, we rarely conclude that the right answer is to have all of one thing or all of another. In fact, we have a special name for these situations—corner solutions—to reflect how unusual they are. Let's take the question of how often to clean your desk. On the one hand, cleaning up takes time, which could be spent working. On the other, clutter eventually makes things hard to find. So how messy should you be?

To BHP CEO Marius Kloppers, the answer was 'perfectly clean'. In 2012, he circulated a memo to staff in BHP's Perth office, banning indoor plants, iPads and smelly food from the workplace.[4] Desks had to be cleaned entirely at the end of the day, with all sticky notes removed from monitors. Sentimental types were firmly instructed that they could have only one photo frame on their desk, provided it was A5 size or smaller.

In effect, Kloppers—a chemical engineer by training—was advocating a corner solution. But for many BHP staff, perfect cleanliness was as inefficient as extreme mess. Seven months after the memo was circulated, Kloppers stepped down as CEO. Ironically, while he was focused on efficiency, a demand for such high levels of cleanliness may have had the effect of reducing productivity.[5] The optimal answer for most of us will be to have a few papers lying around, but not so many that the piles of mouldering paper are at risk of toppling.

Thinking about trade-offs causes economists to reason differently about when their child should start school. At present, one in five children are held back at home for an additional year before starting school. A non-economist might ask: 'is junior ready?' An economist would be more likely to ask: 'which trade-off is better—another year of childhood or another year of work?' Assuming that the child is going to retire at the same age regardless, another year at home means a career that's one year shorter. Oh, and in case you're worrying, the economic evidence seems to point against holding your child back.[6]

Economics can give you the confidence to run against the herd. Popular wisdom might advise that 'winners never quit and quitters never win'—but economists recognise that there are plenty of situations in which quitting is exactly the right thing to do. The error that non-economists often make is 'the fallacy of the sunk cost'—failing to recognise that past decisions cannot be undone. My brother Tim once took six months off his university studies to see if he could make it as a professional cyclist. He rode hundreds of kilometres each week, and began to win more races. But Tim could tell that he wasn't going to make it at the elite level, so quit professional cycling and went back to his studies. As he told me, 'I saw the other riders who would do anything for a professional contract and realised that for me winning a race wasn't everything. To compete at that level it had to be my one and only focus.'

University of Chicago economist Steve Levitt uses the motto 'fail fast' to characterise this approach.[7] Once you recognise that the world is uncertain, you shouldn't be afraid to try plenty of different things, and drop the ones that don't work out. This doesn't just apply in the dating and job markets, but in cultural consumption. Tyler Cowen, who runs *Marginal Revolution*, one of the world's most popular economics blogs, has argued that most of us are too prone to finishing books.[8] You will end your life not having read thousands of delightful books. So why persevere with a bad book when you could simply pop down to the library and try a new one? (You can decide for yourself why I decided to tell you about this in the conclusion rather than the introduction.)

Economists are always looking at people's incentives. We get an oversupply of inaccurate forecasts because public pundits have a stronger incentive to be interesting than to be correct. Plenty of talking heads have been dropped for being boring—but if any have been fired because their predictions turned out to be wrong, I'd like to hear about it. In other areas, experts may be off the mark because their private financial incentives don't align with their incentive to tell the truth. Incentives help explain why you should pay your financial planner a flat fee rather than a commission. They also suggest you should take the ratings of wine experts with a hint of scepticism. For example, one major wine publication was found to have given higher ratings to wines that advertised in the magazine than those that did not.[9] Economists like to ask the old Latin question: *cui bono*—meaning 'to whose benefit?'

Another vital economic tool is cost–benefit analysis. In this book, I've shown how you can use it in places as diverse as ranking the all-time best cricket batsmen, getting to bed earlier and determining the social value of the Australian gun buyback. There are few more powerful tools to help you make good decisions—even on uncomfortable topics. For example, University of Minnesota economist Joel Waldfogel found that Christmas presents are valued at 18 per cent less by the recipient than the price the giver paid for them. Put another way, the typical Christmas gift doesn't pass the cost–benefit test (on a monetary basis, anyway). Because Australians give $6 billion of gifts, the deadweight cost of Christmas is about $1 billion per year.[10] Waldfogel doesn't advocate abolishing Christmas presents, but his results do remind us that we're often not very good at anticipating others' needs. If you don't know Uncle Cedric particularly well, perhaps this Christmas, a gift card or a charitable donation in his name might be more suitable than a novelty tie pin.

Economists are unlikely to be embarrassed about paying other people to do things they could have done themselves. Suppose your favourite pair of pants is torn, and you have to choose whether to fix them yourself or pay someone else to do it. The DIY job would take an hour or you can pay $30 for someone else to fix them. Unless you enjoy sewing, an economist would simply ask: 'is an hour of my time worth $30?' If you can work an hour's overtime and earn $35 after tax, it makes sense to get someone else to do the job.

The notion of comparative advantage tells us that even if the CEO is a fabulous barista, it will still be more efficient for her to pay someone else to make her morning coffee. The question isn't who's best at doing the job, but whether it fits their comparative advantage. Similarly, it makes sense for Australia to be a net importer of clothes and computers, and a net exporter of wheat and university degrees. Australia's comparative advantage lies in things like agriculture and quality education. Other countries' comparative advantage might be in textiles or repetitive factory work.

Behavioural economics teaches us that people tend to be overly focused on today, which makes it hard to lose weight, stop smoking or get more sleep. An excessive focus on the present can lead us to make other errors of judgement too. Economists have shown that people are more likely to purchase a convertible if they test-drive it on a sunny day, and will pay more for a house with a swimming pool if the sale takes place in summer. Conversely, people are more likely to buy black cars on cloudy days and more likely to enrol in a university if they visit its campus on a cloudy day (cloudiness increases the appeal of academic activities). Other studies show that we buy more at the supermarket if we shop on an empty stomach, and are less likely to want to use contraceptives if we're sexually aroused.[11]

One way to make better decisions is to draw on the insights of others. Sure, each of us is unique, but you and I aren't really all that different from one another. Asked 'How similar are you to others', most of us say 'not very'. Yet when the question is posed as 'How similar are others to you?', most of us say 'very'.[12] So why not draw on the 'wisdom of crowds' by reading Amazon ratings, checking out crowd-sourced restaurant reviews, and asking ten friends before you decide what to study?

In this book, I've touched upon dieting and dating, firearms and forecasting, poverty and painting. But while the subject matter changes, the themes stay constant: think about incentives, recognise trade-offs, don't fall for the sunk-cost fallacy, play your comparative advantage and make decisions at the margin. And (because we're all behavioural economists now) acknowledge that you'll probably be time-inconsistent and work out when you might have to lash yourself Odysseus-style to the mast. Now, you're ready to apply economics to just about everything.

Notes

Introduction

1. M. Rowland, 'Women sit tight for $3,000 baby bonus', *PM*, ABC radio, 30 June 2004.

2. Quoted in J. Gans & A. Leigh, 'Born on the First of July: An (un)natural experiment in birth timing', *Journal of Public Economics*, 2009, vol. 93, no. 1–2, pp. 246–63.

3. Gans & Leigh, 2009. 'Born on the First of July'.

4. Gans & Leigh, 'Did the Death of Australian Inheritance Taxes Affect Deaths?', 2006, *The B.E. Journal of Economic Analysis and Policy*, vol. 6, no. 1, pp. 1–9.

5. Gary S. Becker, 1976, *The Economic Approach to Human Behavior*, Chicago: University of Chicago Press, p. 5.

6. A. Deaton, 'Letter from America: Random walks by young economists', *Royal Economic Society Newsletter*, Issue 137, April 2007.

7. See C. Bateson, *The Convict Ships 1787–1868*, 2nd edn, Glasgow: Brown, Son & Ferguson, 1969.

8. J. McDonald & R. Shlomowitz, 'Mortality on Convict Voyages to Australia', *Social Science History*, 1989, vol. 13, no. 3, pp. 285–313. Though important, the change in financial incentives was not the only shift. Another change was that each vessel was required to carry a naval

surgeon. For an extensive discussion, see Bateson, *The Convict Ships*, p. 145.

9. M.K. Chen, V. Lakshminarayanan & L.R. Santos, 'How Basic Are Behavioral Biases? Evidence from capuchin monkey trading behavior', *Journal of Political Economy*, 2006, vol. 114, no. 3, pp. 517–37. See also the earlier work testing price theory on rats and pigeons: J.H. Kagel, R.C. Battalio, H. Rachlin & L. Green, 'Demand Curves for Animal Consumers', *Quarterly Journal of Economics*, 1981, vol. 96, pp. 1–16.

10. My point is about expert economists. But empirically, it does not appear to be true of those who study economics at the undergraduate level. Surveys of economics students conclude that students studying economics were less likely than non-economists to point out an error in their favour, less likely to say that they would return money dropped by a stranger, and less likely to donate money to charity: R.H. Frank, T. Gilovich & D.T. Regan, 'Does Studying Economics Inhibit Cooperation?', *Journal of Economic Perspectives*, 1993, vol. 7, pp. 159–171. And as a Labor MP, I'm a little troubled by a new German study which finds that as economics students proceed through their studies, they are less likely to support the social democrats: N. Potrafke, M. Fischer & H.W. Ursprung, 'Does the Field of Study Influence Students' Political Attitudes?', Paper presented at the 2013 German Economic Association Annual Conference, Dusseldorf, Conference Paper 79934.

11. S.S. Iyengar & M.R. Lepper, 'When Choice is Demotivating: Can one desire too much of a good thing?', *Journal of Personality and Social Psychology*, 2000, vol. 79, no. 6, p. 995; S. Iyengar, *The Art of Choosing*, New York: Twelve, 2010, pp. 180–3, 189–90.

12. The myth was propagated in the 1958 Disney film *White Wilderness*, and debunked in 1982 by the Canadian Broadcasting Corporation's program *The Fifth Estate*. Disney producers used a record turntable near the cliff edge, which flicked the lemmings to their deaths.

13. This example is drawn from D. Ariely, *Predictably Irrational: The hidden forces that shape our decisions*, revised edn, New York: HarperCollins, 2009, p. 152.

Chapter 1: For love or money

1. D. Field, 'Mt Isa Mayor welcomes ugly women', *The World Today*, ABC radio, 18 August 2008; Warrick quoted in S. O'Brien, 'Outrage after mayor's "ugly" behaviour', *The Age*, 18 August 2008.
2. I am grateful to Justin Wolfers for suggesting this analogy. It is also worth noting another margin of adjustment, which is that Mount Isa could have significantly more gay men than lesbian women. To the extent that it is possible to determine sexuality from the Census, the statistics do not support this hypothesis.
3. More dating tips from Australian economists are outlined in J. Irvine, 'Dateonomics', Sunday Life Magazine, *Sun Herald*, 5 August 2012, pp. 12–13.
4. T. Hill, 'Knowing When to Stop', *American Scientist*, 2009, vol. 97, no. 2, p. 126.
5. G.J. Hitsch, A. Hortaçsu & D. Ariely, 'What Makes You Click?—Mate preferences in online dating', *Quantitative Marketing and Economics*, 2010, vol. 8, no. 4, pp. 393–427.
6. G.J. Hitsch, A. Hortaçsu & D. Ariely, 'Matching and Sorting in Online Dating', *American Economic Review*, 2010, vol. 100, no. 1, pp. 130–63.
7. RSVP, *Date of the Nation Report*, 2013, <www.rsvp.com.au>, accessed 24 February 2014.
8. M. Belot & M. Francesconi, *Can Anyone Be 'The' One? Evidence on Mate Selection from Speed Dating*, IZA discussion papers 2377, Bonn: Institute for the Study of Labor (IZA), 2006.
9. R. Fisman, S.S. Iyengar, E. Kamenica & I. Simonson, 'Gender Differences in Mate Selection: Evidence from a speed dating experiment', *Quarterly

Journal of Economics, 2006, vol. 121, no. 2, pp. 673–97. For example, Lin and Lundquist found that white men and white women with a university degree were more likely to contact and respond to a white dater without a degree than a black dater with a degree: K.-H. Lin & J. Lundquist, 'Mate Selection in Cyberspace: The intersection of race, gender, and education', *American Journal of Sociology*, 2013, vol. 119, no. 1, pp. 183–215.

10. B. Stevenson & J. Wolfers, 'Marriage and Divorce: Changes and their driving forces', *Journal of Economic Perspectives*, 2007, vol. 21, no. 2, pp. 27–52.

11. B. Stevenson & J. Wolfers, 'Economic Growth and Subjective Well-Being: Reassessing the Easterlin paradox', *Brookings Papers on Economic Activity*, 2008, vol. 39, no. 1, pp. 1–102.

12. Homer, *The Odyssey* [800BCE] (1752), translated by Alexander Pope, London: Henry Lintot, Book 12.

13. Forty-six per cent of divorces are initiated by women, 24 per cent by men, and 30 per cent are a joint decision.

14. My analysis used data from the Household, Income and Labour Dynamics in Australia (HILDA) survey, and was based on taking those who were married in 2002 and comparing individuals who were married in 2003–2007 with those who were divorced or separated in at least one of those years. The exercise is inspired by Betsey Stevenson's 'divorce calculator' for the United States, *divorce360*, <www.divorce360.com/content/divorcecalculator.aspx>, accessed 24 February 2014. HILDA was initiated and is funded by the Australian Government Department of Social Services and is managed by the Melbourne Institute of Applied Economic and Social Research. Neither organisation is responsible for the conclusions in this book.

15. A. Leigh, 'Does Child Gender Affect Marital Status? Evidence from Australia', *Journal of Population Economics*, 2009, vol. 22, no. 2, pp. 351–66.

16. Rates of sex-selective abortion in Australia are likely to be low: see Leigh, 'Does Child Gender Affect Marital Status?'.

17. B. Phillips, J. Li & M. Taylor, (2013), *Cost of Kids: The cost of raising children in Australia*. AMP.NATSEM Income and Wealth Report, no. 33, Sydney: AMP, May 2013. The estimate is $812,043 for a middle-income family, in 2011–12 dollars, which still rounds to $800,000 after accounting for inflation since then.

18. Using 2001 data, one study puts the cost of two children at $350,000: T. Breusch & E. Gray, 'New Estimates of Mothers' Forgone Earnings Using HILDA Data', *Australian Journal of Labour Economics*, 2004, vol. 7, no. 2, pp. 125–150. From 2001 to 2013, average female full-time ordinary time earnings grew by 70 per cent, so I scale this up to $600,000 (rounded to the nearest hundred thousand dollars).

19. Australian Bureau of Statistics, 'Same-sex Couple Families', *Reflecting a Nation: Stories from the 2011 Census, 2012–2013*, Cat. no. 2071.0, Canberra: ABS, 2012; Australian Bureau of Statistics, *Australian Social Trends—Same-sex couples*, Cat. no. 4102.0, Canberra: ABS, 2013.

20. D. Black, G. Gates, S. Saunders & L. Taylor, 'Why Do Gay Men Live in San Francisco?', *Journal of Urban Economics*, 2002, vol. 51, no. 1, pp. 54–76. While the authors focus only on gay men, their results are similar for lesbian women. In the interests of inclusiveness, I focus on both. The idea of applying this theory to Australia first came about through an opinion article that I wrote with Justin Wolfers: A. Leigh & J. Wolfers, 2002, 'If That City's Where the Boys Are, Then It Has To Be Fabulous', *Sydney Morning Herald*, 13 May 2002. Statistics on the share of same-sex couples in Australian cities are from Australian Bureau of Statistics, 'Same-sex Couple Families'.

21. Dan Ariely uses this example to discuss the difference between market and non-market norms: D. Ariely, *Predictably Irrational: The hidden forces that shape our decisions*, revised edn, New York: HarperCollins, 2009, pp. 100–1.

Chapter 2: Fit for tomorrow

1. This account is drawn from 'The Biggest Winner', *Australian Story*, ABC television, broadcast 3 July 2007.

2. This example is drawn from D. Laibson, 2010, 'Empirical evidence on quasi-hyperbolic discounting', lecture delivered at the American Economic Association meetings, Atlanta, GA, January 2010.

3. D. Read & B. van Leeuwen, 'Predicting Hunger: The effects of appetite and delay on choice', *Organizational Behavior and Human Decision Processes*, 1998, vol. 76, no. 2, pp. 189–205. The authors do not provide overall averages, so the figures I quote here are based on averaging the subgroup results in their Figure 1.

4. M.M. Scollo & M.H. Winstanley, *Tobacco in Australia: Facts and issues*, 4th edn, Melbourne: Cancer Council Victoria, 2012, Chapter 1.3, <www.TobaccoInAustralia.org.au>, accessed 24 February 2014.

5. R. Klein, *Cigarettes are Sublime*, Durham, NC: Duke University Press, 1994, p. 105.

6. R. Borland & J. Balmford, 'Understanding How Mass Media Campaigns Impact on Smokers', *Tobacco Control*, 2003, vol. 12, pp. ii45–ii52. Respondents were asked whether they were happy to smoke (8 per cent), or 'Should quit sometime, not soon', 'Open to possibility', 'Considering quitting, not in next 30 days', 'Planning, not in next two weeks', 'Quit date within next two weeks' (totalling 92 per cent).

7. For the cost of cigarettes, see Scollo & Winstanley, *Tobacco in Australia*, ch. 13.3; for a review of the relevant studies on the effect of prices, see D.M. Cutler & E.L. Glaeser, 'Why Do Europeans Smoke More Than Americans?', in D. Wise (ed.), *Developments in the Economics of Aging*, Chicago: University of Chicago Press, 2009, pp. 255–82.

8. Tobacco advertisements on radio and television were banned in 1976, and tobacco advertisements in newspapers were banned in 1990: Scollo & Winstanley, *Tobacco in Australia*, ch. 11; D. Germain,

M.A. Wakefield & S.J. Durkin, 'Adolescents' Perceptions of Cigarette Brand Image: Does plain packaging make a difference?', *Journal of Adolescent Health*, vol. 46, no. 4, 2010, pp. 385–92.

9. Cutler & Glaeser, 'Why Do Europeans Smoke More Than Americans?'; Scollo & Winstanley, *Tobacco in Australia*, ch. 3.34.

10. Australian National Preventive Health Agency, *State of Preventive Health 2013*, Report to the Australian Government Minister for Health, Canberra: ANPHA, 2013, pp. 58–60.

11. X. Gin, D. Karlan & J. Zinman, 'Put Your Money Where Your Butt Is: A commitment contract for smoking cessation,' *American Economic Journal: Applied Economics*, 2010, vol. 2, no. 4, pp. 213–35.

12. B. Smee & N. Davidson, 'Tears for Alana and Stephanie', *Newcastle Herald*, 13 January 2011.

13. New South Wales Government Bureau of Transport Statistics, 'NSW and Sydney Transport Facts', Sydney: Bureau of Transport Statistics, 2012. The estimate is based upon multiplying the average travel time per weekday (78 minutes) by the number of weekdays per year (260).

14. Seatbelts were compulsory in Victoria from 1970, in New South Wales, South Australia, Western Australia and Tasmania from 1971, and in the other jurisdictions from 1972; both random breath-testing and speed cameras were first used in Victoria; 50 km/h residential speed limits were first trialled by New South Wales in 1997, and Queensland in 1999; for example, driving 35 km/h over the speed limit in Queensland earned a fine of $180 in early 2003, but $513 by late 2013: more than double even after inflation (in New South Wales, the same offence attracts a penalty of $815—or $1028 in a school zone).

15. S. Peltzman, 'The Effects of Automobile Safety Regulation', *Journal of Political Economy*, 1975, vol. 83, no. 4, pp. 677–725; S. Dickert-Conlin, T. Elder & B. Moore, 'Donorcycles: Motorcycle Helmet Laws and the Supply of Organ Donors', *Journal of Law and Economics*, 2011, vol. 54, no. 4, pp. 907–35.

16. Australian Bureau of Statistics, 'Accidents, Injuries and Fatalities', *Year Book Australia*, Cat no. 1301.0, Canberra: ABS, 2012. These figures include deaths of pedestrians and cyclists.

17. Figure for 1980 from A. Leigh, 'Safer for Owners, Not for Others', *Canberra Times*, 4 July 2003; the latest estimate is 30 per cent from Australian Bureau of Statistics, *Sales of New Motor Vehicles, Australia*, Cat. no. 9314.0, Canberra: ABS, 2013. That source includes data back to 1994, when just 7 per cent of new vehicles sold were SUVs.

18. Crash statistics from S. Newstead, L. Watson & M. Cameron, *Vehicle Safety Ratings Estimated from Police Reported Crash Data: 2011 Update*, Monash University Accident Research Centre report 304, Melbourne: Monash University, 2011, pp. 27, 37.

19. M. White, 'The "Arms Race" on American Roads: The Effect of Sport Utility Vehicles and Pickup Trucks on Traffic Safety', *Journal of Law and Economics*, 2004, vol. XLVII, no. 2, pp. 333–56.

20. Data for 1980 and 1990s extracted from the OECD Statistics database, available at <http://stats.oecd.org/>, accessed 24 February 2014. Recent figures are for 2011–12, drawn from Australian National Preventive Health Agency, *State of Preventive Health 2013*, p. 46; weight gain per decade from M.M. Finucane, G.A. Stevens, M.J. Cowan, G. Danaei, J.K. Lin, C.J. Paciorek, G.M. Singh et al., 'National, Regional, and Global Trends in Body-mass Index Since 1980: systematic analysis of health examination surveys and epidemiological studies with 960 country-years and 9.1 million participants', *Lancet*, 2011, vol. 377, no. 9765, pp. 557–67.

21. For an explanation of trends prior to 1970, see T. Philipson & R. Posner, 'The Long Run Growth of Obesity as a Function of Technological Change', *Perspectives in Biology and Medicine*, 2003, vol. 46, no. 3, pp. 87–108. The authors argue that the shift towards more sedentary jobs applies across a broader timeframe, but subsequent work has shown that it is largely confined to the pre-1970 era. D.M. Cutler, E.L. Glaeser & J.M. Shapiro, 'Why

Have Americans Become More Obese?', *Journal of Economic Perspectives*, 2003, vol. 17, no. 3, pp. 93–118. In the US case, the growth in BMI from 1970 onwards would require the average American to have reduced their energy consumption by the equivalent of walking two kilometres per day. The time-use surveys do not show any such shift.

22. For example, Nutrition Australia recommends a daily intake for women of 9300 kJ (ages 19–50) and 8800 kJ (ages 51–70). For men, they recommend 11,500 kJ (ages 19–50) and 10,450 kJ (ages 51–70). On changes in actual intakes, see M.A. Allman-Farinelli, T. Chey, A.E. Bauman, T. Gill & W.P.T. James, 'Age, Period and Birth Cohort Effects on Prevalence of Overweight and Obesity in Australian Adults from 1990 to 2000', *European Journal of Clinical Nutrition*, 2007, vol. 62, no. 7, pp. 898–907.

23. For a discussion of the role of carbohydrates in weight gain, see G. Taubes, *Why We Get Fat and What To Do About It*, New York: Anchor Books, 2011.

24. It's worth noting that these technological changes have not altered the relative price of healthy versus unhealthy foods. See J.B. Gelbach, J. Klick & T. Stratmann, 'Cheap Donuts and Expensive Broccoli: The Effect of Relative Prices on Obesity', 2007, Florida State University College of Law Public Law Research Paper 261, Tallahassee, FL: Florida State University College of Law.

25. Cutler, Glaeser & Shapiro, 'Why Have Americans Become More Obese?'.

26. According to a 2012 Nielsen Global Survey, 56 per cent of Australians are actively trying to lose weight: Neilsen, 'The Heavy Country: Two-thirds of Australians think they are overweight', 21 February 2012, <www.nielsen.com>, accessed 24 February 2014.

27. Other dieting tips from Australian economists are detailed in D. Macken, 'No Sugar! I'm an economist', *Australian Financial Review*, 21–22 April 2012, pp. 52–3.

28. B. Wansink, D.R. Just & C.R. Payne, 'Mindless eating and healthy heuristics for the irrational', *American Economic Review*, 2009, vol. 99, no. 2,

pp. 165–69; M. Bertrand & D.W. Schanzenbach, 'Time use and food consumption', *American Economic Review*, 2009, vol. 99, no. 2, pp. 170–6; B. Wansink & J.-Y. Kim, 'Bad Popcorn in Big Buckets: Portion size can influence intake as much as taste', *Journal of Nutrition Education and Behavior*, 2005, vol. 37, no. 5, pp. 242–5.

29. Wansink, Just & Payne, 'Mindless eating and healthy heuristics for the irrational'.

30. Quoted in S. Mullainathan & E. Shafir, *Scarcity: Why having too little means so much*, New York: Macmillan, 2013, p. 60.

31. D.J. Bartlett, N.S. Marshall, A. Williams & R.R. Grunstein, 'Sleep Health New South Wales: Chronic sleep restriction and daytime sleepiness', *Internal Medicine Journal*, 2008, vol. 38, no. 1, pp. 24–31.

32. H. Tattersall, 'Toiling Towards an Early Grave', *Australian Financial Review*, 22 July 2008, p. 59.

33. J.E. Biddle & D.S. Hamermesh, 'Sleep and the Allocation of Time', *Journal of Political Economy*, 1990, vol. 98, no. 5, part 1, pp. 922–43.

34. T. Lange, B. Perras, H.L. Fehm & J. Born, 'Sleep Enhances the Human Antibody Response to Hepatitis A Vaccination', *Psychosomatic Medicine*, 2003, vol. 65, no. 5, pp. 831–5.

35. C. Anderson & D.L. Dickinson, 'Bargaining and Trust: The effects of 36-h total sleep deprivation on socially interactive decisions', *Journal of Sleep Research*, 2010, vol. 19, no. 1, part I, pp. 54–63; T.H. Turner, S.P.A. Drummond, J.S. Salamat & G.G. Brown, 'Effects of 42 hr of Total Sleep Deprivation on Component Processes of Verbal Working Memory', *Neuropsychology*, 2007, vol. 21, no. 6, pp. 787–95; S.-S. Yoo, N. Gujar, P. Hu, F.A. Jolesz & M.P. Walker, 'The Human Emotional Brain without Sleep—A prefrontal amygdala disconnect', *Current Biology*, 2007, vol. 17, no. 20, pp. R877–R878; truck driver quoted in A. Albanese, 'Long, Dangerous Road to Fair Go for Truckies', *Daily Telegraph*, 20 February 2012, p. 23. One estimate puts the annual cost of sleep deprivation in Australia at $5.1 billion: D.R. Mansfield, D.R. Hillman, N.A. Antic, R.D. McEvoy

& S.M. Rajaratnam, 'Sleep loss and sleep disorders', *Medical Journal of Australia*, 2013, vol. 199, no. 8, pp. 5-6.

36. Australian Transport Council, *National Road Safety Strategy 2011–2020*, Canberra: ATC, 2011, p. 25.

37. K.M. Murphy & R.H. Topel, 'The Value of Health and Longevity', *Journal of Political Economy*, 2006, vol. 114, no. 4, pp. 871-904; life expectancy and income figures from Australian Bureau of Statistics, *Measures of Australia's Progress: Summary Indicators, 2011*, Cat. no. 1370.0.5.001. Canberra: ABS, 2011.

38. E. Feletto, F. Sitas, A. Gibberd, C. Kahn, M. Weber, P. Grogan et al., *The State of Cancer Control in Australia: Cancer Council NSW research report summary*, Sydney: Cancer Council NSW, 2013.

Chapter 3: Starting lineup

1. *Australian Story*, 'Suddenly Last Summer', ABC TV, broadcast 11 March 2013, including the quote from cricket writer Peter Lalor.

2. Malcolm Knox, 2006, 'Making the Pitch', *The Guardian*, 29 October 2006; Gideon Haigh, quoted in *Australian Story*, 'Suddenly Last Summer', ABC TV, broadcast 11 March 2013.

3. N. Rohde, 'An "Economic" Ranking of Batters in Test Cricket', *Economic Papers: A Journal of Applied Economics and Policy*, 2011, vol. 30, no. 4, pp. 455–65 (the published ranking ended in 31 December 2010, but Nicholas Rohde kindly provided me with updated rankings to 24 November 2013). Specifically, for each innings Rohde subtracts the batting average of all batsmen (ie. players batting in positions one to four) who played in that year. This ensures that a player's ranking increases in innings when he plays better than the average batsman of his era, and decreases in innings when his performance is lower.

4. E. Bledsoe (ed.), *Getting Naked with Harry Crews: Interviews*, Miami: University of Florida Press, 1999.

5. P. Kent, 'Four Players Sin-binned Following Dramatic Fight in State of Origin Game II', *Daily Telegraph*, 26 June 2013.

6. Accounts of State of Origin fights are legion. See for example P. Lutton, 'Origin's Best Biffo', *Brisbane Times*, 16 July 2009; S. Ricketts, B. Dick & P. Malone, 'The 30 Greatest Controversies in 30 Years of State of Origin Series', *Courier-Mail*, 23 May 2012.

7. K. Belson, 2013, 'N.F.L. Agrees To Settle Concussion Suit for $765 Million', *New York Times*, 30 August 2013; For comparative statistics on AFL and league attendances, see A. Leigh, *Disconnected*, Sydney: University of New South Wales Press, 2010.

8. S. Aiyar & R. Ramcharan, *What Can International Cricket Teach Us About the Role of Luck in Labor Markets?*, IMF Working Paper 10/225, IMF: Washington DC, 2010. The authors performed several tests to show that debuting at home or abroad is random. For example, they pointed out that, of *Wisden*'s top ten batsmen of the twentieth century, five debuted at home and five debuted abroad.

9. J. Fingleton, *Brightly Fades the Don*, Sydney and London: Collins, 1949, p. 198. The calculation of Bradman's average if there had been no war is based on unpublished estimates from Bruce Chapman. Chapman estimated that in the period 1939–45, Bradman's average was 102.75. Over the four 'missing' tests, Bradman would have played an additional 28 innings, which would have increased his career average from 99.94 to 100.74. See N. Gruen, 'Bradman's Average Hits 100—Shock!', Club Troppo, <http://clubtroppo.com.au/2007/07/06/bradmans-average-should-have-been-100-shock/>, accessed 22 February 2014.

10. L. Page & M. Schaffner, 2013, 'Outcome Bias in Performance Evaluation: Evidence from a natural experiment', working draft, Queensland University of Technology, Brisbane, 15 July 2013.

11. The Sheffield Shield sample includes 149 players. Most youth cricket competitions use a cut-off age of 31 August or 1 September, though the Toyota Futures League uses 30 June. There are 570 players in the NRL

sample. Most school Rugby League competitions use 1 January as the cut-off date. At the time of writing, the Matildas squad was 20 players, while the Socceroos squad was 22 players. The FIFA cut-off for youth soccer is 1 August.

12. For an analysis of related data on Australian sporting teams (which finds age effects for AFL, cricket and Rugby League, but not soccer and Rugby Union), see A.B. Abernethy & D. Farrow, 'Contextual factors influencing the development of expertise in Australian athletes', in Tony Morris, Peter C. Terry, Sandy Gordon, Stephanie Hanrahan, Lydia Ievleva, Gregory Kolt and P. Tremayne, *ISSP 2005: Promoting Health and Performance for Life. Refereed Proceedings of the ISSP 11th World Congress of Sport Psychology*. ISSP 11th World Congress of Sport Psychology: Promoting Health and Performance for Life, Sydney, 15–19 August 2005. See also A.G. Barnett, 'The Relative Age Effect in Australian Football League Players', Working Paper, Brisbane: Queensland University of Technology, 2010. A very entertaining discussion also appears in M. Gladwell, *Outliers: The Story of Success*, New York: Little, Brown and Company, 2008.

13. J. Musch & R. Hay, 'The Relative Age Effect in Soccer: Cross-cultural evidence for a systematic discrimination against children born late in the competition year', *Sociology of Sport Journal*, 1999, vol. 16, no. 1, pp. 54–64.

14. The calculation of wins is for the regular 22-game season, and excludes finals matches. Draws are treated the same as losses. Expenditure estimates include player expenditure and operating expenditure, and are drawn from annual reports. Five teams' expenditure data are incomplete for 2012, so I assume their 2011 expenditure increased at the same rate as for the other 11 teams (8 percent). All expenditure data is then converted to 2013 dollars and summed across the five-year period. Formally, the relationship between AFL club expenditure and wins in the period 2008–2012 is: Wins = $-45.3 + 1.1 \times$ Expenditure ($t = 2.02$), with

an R-squared of 0.23. The R-squared is slightly lower when using the log of expenditure.

15. For an account of Wells' success, see J. Ralph, 'Master Geelong Recruiter Stephen Wells Can't Dodge the Plaudits', *Herald Sun*, 17 November 2013. I am grateful to Richard Marles for drawing Wells' role to my attention. Jeff Borland's view is that Geelong's success is also attributable to having a CEO (Brian Cook), football director (Neil Balme) and coaches (Mark Thompson and Chris Scott) rated among the best in the AFL.

16. There is an economic literature on this point: see e.g. A.B. Bernard & M.R. Busse, 'Who Wins the Olympic Games: Economic resources and medal totals', *Review of Economics and Statistics*, 2004, vol. 86, no. 1, pp. 413–17; H.-K. Lui & W. Suen, 'Men, Money, and Medals: An econometric analysis of the Olympic Games', *Pacific Economic Review*, 2008, vol. 13, no. 1, pp. 1–16.

17. More than 200 'National Olympic Committees' were represented at the 2012 Olympics.

18. Data from *Medals Per Capita: Olympic glory in proportion*, <www.medalspercapita.com>, accessed 22 February 2013, which contains many fascinating comparisons. The relationship between GDP and Olympic medals in 2012 is: Wins = 5.1 + 0.008 × GDP (t = 13.4), with an R-squared of 0.68. The R-squared is slightly lower when using the log of GDP.

19. When I put them both into log terms, population and GDP per capita have approximately equal impacts on medal counts. A 10 per cent increase in GDP per capita is associated with 0.5 more medals, while a 10 per cent increase in population is associated with 0.6 more medals.

20. The formula for the expected number of heads or tails in a row is equal to $-\log n(1-p)/\log p$, where n is the number of seasons and p is the probability of a win. Because the comparison is with an evenly balanced contest, I set $p = 0.5$ in all calculations. See M.F. Schilling, 'The Surprising Predictability of Long Runs', *Mathematics Magazine*, 2012, vol. 85,

no. 2, pp. 141–9. The Ashes series wins were England from 1882–83 to 1890 (eight series in a row) and Australia from 1989 to 2002–03 (eight in a row). If we treat retaining the Ashes as a win, there are two other series lasting over five series: Australia from 1934 to 1950–51 (six in a row) and Australia from 1958–59 to 1968 (six in a row). Overall, Australia and England have each won 31 series, with five drawn.

21. The series of Bledisloe Cup wins stretching longer than five years are New Zealand 1951–78 (12 series in a row) and 2003–13 (11 series in a row). The former stands if we include years in which both teams won the same number of games (in which case the Cup does not change hands). The latter succession of victories does not stand on this basis. The series of State of Origin wins (both by Queensland) are 1980–84 (five series wins in a row) and 2006–13 (eight series wins in a row). In total, Queensland has won 20 series and New South Wales 12, with two draws. The predecessor series to State of Origin was even less competitive, with New South Wales winning all series in the 1960s and 1970s. I am grateful for Tim Watts for drawing this point to my attention.

22. I refer to 'alleged' tanking since no team has ever been prosecuted for tanking, and an economics study that analysed AFL results from 1968 to 2005 found no definitive evidence of tanking: J. Borland, M. Chicu & R.D. Macdonald, 'Do Teams Always Lose To Win? Performance incentives and the player draft in the Australian Football League', *Journal of Sports Economics*, 2009, vol. 10, no. 5, pp. 451–84. The improvement of competitive balance in NRL and AFL since 1985 is documented in R. Booth, 'Comparing Competitive Balance in Australian Sports Leagues: Does a salary cap and player draft measure up?', *Sport Management Review*, 2005, vol. 8, no. 2, pp. 119–143. Comparing codes, Booth concluded that within-season competitive balance is higher in the NRL than AFL. Another study reaches the same conclusion, finding that the AFL is more competitive on a between-season

basis: L.J.A. Lenten, 'Towards a New Dynamic Measure of Competitive Balance: A study applied to Australia's two major professional "football" leagues', *Economic Analysis and Policy*, 2009, vol. 39, no. 3, pp. 407–28.

23. S.M. Crowe & J. Middeldorp, 'A comparison of leg before wicket rates between Australians and their visiting teams for test cricket series played in Australia, 1977–94', 1996, *Statistician*, vol. 45, no. 2, pp. 255–62; P.B. Mohr & K. Larsen, 'Ingroup Favoritism in Umpiring Decisions in Australian Football', *Journal of Social Psychology*, 1998, vol. 138, no. 4, pp. 495–504; L. Page & K. Page, *Evidence of Referees' National Favouritism in Rugby*, NCER Working Paper 62, Brisbane: National Centre for Econometric Research, Queensland University of Technology: Brisbane, 2010; P. Downward & M. Jones, 'Effects of Crowd Size on Referee Decisions: Analysis of the FA Cup', *Journal of Sports Sciences*, 2007, vol. 25, no. 14, pp. 1541–5; T.J. Dohmen, 'The Influence of Social Forces: Evidence from the behavior of football referees', *Economic Inquiry*, 2008, vol. 46, no. 3, pp. 411–24; R.H. Boyko, A.R. Boyko & M.G. Boyko, 'Referee Bias Contributes to Home Advantage in English Premiership Football', *Journal of Sports Sciences*, 2007, vol. 25, no. 11, pp. 1185–94 (interestingly, while large crowds are associated with an increase in the umpire's home-team bias, one study suggested that an increase in crowd size in baseball leads to less *racial* bias by the umpire: C.A. Parsons, J. Sulaeman, M.C. Yates & D.S. Hamermesh, 'Strike Three: Discrimination, incentives, and evaluation', *American Economic Review*, 2011, vol. 101, no. 4, pp. 1410–35); A.M. Nevill, N.J. Balmer & A.M. Williams, 'The Influence of Crowd Noise and Experience upon Refereeing Decisions in Football', *Psychology of Sport and Exercise*, 2002, vol. 3, no. 4, pp. 261–72.

24. K. Page & L. Page, 'Alone against the Crowd: Individual differences in referees' ability to cope under pressure', *Journal of Economic Psychology*, 2010, vol. 31, no. 2, pp. 192–9.

25. U. Wilbert-Lampen, D. Leistner, S. Greven, T. Pohl, S. Sper, C. Völker et al., 'Cardiovascular Events During World Cup Soccer', *New England Journal of Medicine*, 2008, vol. 358, no. 5, pp. 475–83.

26. P.C. Bernhardt, J.M. Dabbs Jr, J.A. Fielden & C.D. Lutter, 'Testosterone Changes During Vicarious Experiences of Winning and Losing among Fans at Sporting Events', *Physiology and Behavior*, 1998, vol. 65, no. 1, pp. 59–62.

27. The line was used by UCLA coach Henry Sanders in the 1940s to describe American football and more recently by former Liverpool coach Bill Shankly to describe English football.

28. V. Bhaskar, 'Rational Adversaries? Evidence from randomised trials in one day cricket', *Economic Journal*, 2009, vol. 119, no. 534, pp. 1–23.

Chapter 4: Looking for a raise

1. From OECD Stat, 'Average annual hours actually worked per worker' (2012 estimate for Australia), <stats.oecd.org>, accessed 24 February 2014.

2. R. Cassells, A. Duncan, A. Abello, G. D'Souza & B. Nepal, 'Smart Australians: Education and innovation in Australia', *AMP.NATSEM Income and Wealth Report*, October 2012, no. 32.

3. A. Leigh, & C. Ryan, 'Estimating Returns to Education Using Different Natural Experiment Techniques', *Economics of Education Review*, 2008, vol. 27, no. 2, pp. 149–60; P. Oreopoulos, 'Do Dropouts Drop Out Too Soon? Wealth, health and happiness from compulsory schooling', *Journal of Public Economics*, 2007, vol. 91, no. 11, pp. 2213–29.

4. A. Leigh & C. Ryan, 'Long-Run Trends in School Productivity: Evidence from Australia', *Education Finance and Policy*, 2011, vol. 6, no. 1, pp. 105–35. There were five multiple-choice options (2 higher, 1 higher, same, 1 lower, 2 lower). The percentages answering correctly in each year the question was fielded were 1964 88%; 1978 83%; 1995 74%; 1999 74%; and 2003 68%.

5. S. Thomson, L. De Bortoli and S. Buckley, *PISA in Brief: Highlights from the full Australian report*, Melbourne: Australian Council for Educational Research, 2013.

6. C. Ryan, 'What is Behind the Decline in Student Achievement in Australia?', *Economics of Education Review*, 2013, vol. 37, pp. 226–39. See also E. Gundlach, L. Wossmann & J. Gmelin, 'The Decline of Schooling Productivity in OECD Countries', *Economic Journal*, 2001, vol. 111, no. 471, pp. 135–47.

7. The wage effects of another 10 cm of height are 2.8 per cent for men and 1.5 per cent for women (not statistically significant). Average weekly total earnings for full-time workers are $1606 per week for men, and $1268 for women: Australian Bureau of Statistics, 2013, *Average Weekly Earnings, Australia, May 2013*, Cat. no. 6302.0, ABS, Canberra.

8. P. Wilson, 'Perceptual Distortion of Height as a Function of Ascribed Academic Status', *Journal of Social Psychology*, 1968, vol. 74, no. 1, pp. 97–102. The average estimated heights by ascribed academic status were: student 5 feet 9.9 inches (1.77 m), demonstrator 5 feet 10.14 inches (1.78 m), lecturer 5 feet 10.9 inches (1.80 m), senior lecturer 5 feet 11.6 inches (1.82 m) and professor 6 feet 0.3 inches (1.84 m).

9. N. Persico, A. Postlewaite & D. Silverman, 'The Effect of Adolescent Experience on Labor Market Outcomes: The case of height', *Journal of Political Economy*, 2004, vol. 112, no. 5, pp. 1019–53

10. Gross mean household income is $1847 per week: Australian Bureau of Statistics, *Household Income and Income Distribution, Australia, 2011–12*, Cat. no 6523.0, Canberra: ABS, 2013, Table 7.

11. On Australian anti-discrimination law, see Y. Redrup, 'Ugly People to the Back: Secrets of restaurant seating plans', *Crikey*, 14 November 2013. On US anti-discrimination law, see 'Hiring Hotties', *The Economist*, 21 July 2012. In Iowa (a jurisdiction without a ban on beauty discrimination), an employer was allowed to fire an employee for being too beautiful: M. Kimmel, 'Fired for Being Beautiful', *New York Times*, 16 July 2013.

For women, there is some evidence that even attractive women should not attach photographs to their CV: see 'Don't Hate Me Because I'm Beautiful', *The Economist*, 31 March 2012.

12. K. Schilt & M. Wiswall, 'Before and After: Gender transitions, human capital, and workplace experiences', *B.E. Journal of Economic Analysis & Policy*, 2008, vol. 8, no. 1 (Contributions), Article 39.

13. This is based on an analysis of hourly wages, from J.D. Barón & D.A. Cobb-Clark, 'Occupational Segregation and the Gender Wage Gap in Private- and Public-Sector Employment: A distributional analysis', *Economic Record*, 2010, vol. 86, no. 273, pp. 227–46. A similar picture emerges when comparing wages of full-time workers. For example, a summary of the gender earnings gap among full-time workers finds that it fluctuated between 15 and 18 per cent over the period 1994–2012: Workplace Gender Equality Agency, 'Gender pay gap statistics', Canberra: WGEA, February 2013, <www.wgea.gov.au>. 'Low-paid workers' are those at the 10th percentile; 'high-paid workers' are those at the 90th percentile. Barón & Cobb-Clark, 'Occupational Segregation'. In the public sector, the gender pay gap is similar across the distribution. In most European nations, the gender wage gap is higher at the top of the distribution than the bottom: W. Arulampalam, A.L. Booth & M.L. Bryan, 'Is There a Glass Ceiling over Europe? Exploring the gender pay gap across the wage distribution', *Industrial and Labor Relations Review*, 2007, vol. 60, no. 2, pp. 163–86.

14. Barón & Cobb-Clark, 'Occupational Segregation'. Other research (using a smaller sample) comes to a similar conclusion: see H. Kee, 'Glass Ceiling or Sticky Floor? Exploring the Australian gender pay gap', *Economic Record*, 2006, vol. 82, pp. 408–27.

15. A. Booth & Leigh, 'Do Employers Discriminate by Gender? A field experiment in female-dominated occupations', *Economics Letters*, 2010, vol. 107, no. 2, pp. 236–8.

16. Equal Opportunity for Women in the Workplace Agency, *2012 Australian Census of Women in Leadership*, Canberra: Australian Government,

2012; barrister data from C. Merritt, 'State Raises the Bar on Female Silks', *The Australian*, 7 December 2012; professor data from C. Milburn, 'Beating on the Boys' Club Door', *The Age*, 1 March 2011; Victorian Equal Opportunity and Human Rights Commission, *Changing the Rules: the experiences of female lawyers in Victoria*, Melbourne: VEOHRC, 2012.

17. M. Niederle & L. Vesterlund, 'Do Women Shy Away from Competition? Do Men Compete Too Much?', *Quarterly Journal of Economics*, 2007, 122, no. 3, pp. 1067–101. (A more recent study failed to replicate this specific result: C.R. Price, 'Do Women Shy Away From Competition? Do Men Compete Too Much?: A (failed) replication', 2010, Working Paper, University of Southern Indiana, Evansville, IN.). But other studies find similar patterns: for a review, see R. Croson & U. Gneezy, 'Gender Differences in Preferences', *Journal of Economic Literature*, 2009, vol. 47, no. 2, pp. 448–74.

18. U. Gneezy & A. Rustichini, 'Gender and Competition at a Young Age', *American Economic Review*, 2004, vol. 94, no. 2, pp. 377–81.

19. J. Knight, Sexual stereotypes.' *Nature*, 2002, vol. 415, no. 6869, pp. 254–6.

20. U. Gneezy, K.L. Leonard & J.A. List, 'Gender Differences in Competition: Evidence from a matrilineal and a patriarchal society', *Econometrica*, 2009, vol. 77, no. 5, pp. 1637–64.

21. A. Booth & P. Nolen, 'Choosing to Compete: How different are girls and boys?', *Journal of Economic Behavior & Organization*, 2012, vol. 81, no. 2, pp. 542–55; A.L. Booth & P. Nolen, 'Gender Differences in Risk Behaviour: Does nurture matter?', *Economic Journal*, 2012, vol. 122, no. 558, pp. F56–F78.

22. A. Booth, 'Gender, Risk, and Competition', *VOX: Research-based policy analysis and commentary from leading economists*, blog, 14 September 2009, <www.voxeu.org/article/gender-risk-and-competition-experimental-evidence-environmental-influences>, accessed 22 February 2014.

23. R.B. McIntyre, C.G. Lord, D.M. Gresky, L.L. Ten Eyck, G.D. Jay Frye & C.F. Bond Jr, 'A Social Impact Trend in the Effects of Role Models on

Alleviating Women's Mathematics Stereotype Threat', *Current Research in Social Psychology*, 2005, vol. 10, no. 9, pp. 116–36.

24. Australian Human Rights Commission, *Working Without Fear: Results of the Sexual Harassment National Telephone Survey 2012*, Sydney: AHRC, 2012. The rate of sexual harassment for men was 16 per cent. See e.g. K.T. Schneider, S. Swan & L.F. Fitzgerald, 'Job-Related and Psychological Effects of Sexual Harassment in the Workplace: Empirical evidence from two organizations', *Journal of Applied Psychology*, 1997, vol. 82, no. 3, pp. 401–515; L.F. Fitzgerald & A.J. Ormerod, 'Breaking Silence: The sexual harassment of women in academia and the workplace', in F.L. Denmark & M.A. Paludi (eds), *Psychology of Women: A Handbook of Issues and Theories*, Westport, Conn.: Greenwood Press, 1993; International Labour Office, *Combating Sexual Harassment at Work: Conditions of Work Digest*, vol. 11, no. 1, Geneva: ILO, 1992. See also D.A. Cobb-Clark, 'That Pesky Problem of Persistent Gender Bias', *Australian Economic Review*, 2012, vol. 45, no. 2, pp. 211–15.

25. A. Marshall, *Principles of Economics*, London: Macmillan & Company, 1890, p. 332.

26. This is based on the 2001–2010 HILDA survey. I estimate a regression with person fixed effects, controlling for the following time-varying factors: marital status, having children, school completion, university completion, and a quadratic in age. The sample is people aged 25–64, using longitudinal person weights. Moving to an outer-urban area boosts annual income by 4 per cent. If log hourly wages in place of log annual income are used, moving to a city boosts wages by 7 per cent, and moving to an outer-urban area boosts wages by 4 per cent.

27. If log hourly wages are used in place of log annual income, a 10 per cent increase in the share of the population with university degrees boosts wages by 2 per cent.

28. E. Glaeser, *Triumph of the City: How our greatest invention makes us richer, smarter, greener, healthier and happier*, New York: Pan

Macmillan, 2011. See also E. Glaeser & A. Saiz, 'The Rise of the Skilled City.' *Brookings-Wharton Papers on Urban Affairs*, 2004, vol. 2004, no. 1, pp. 47–105.

29. This assumes lifetime earnings that are a little over $2 million. See Cassells, Duncan, Abello, D'Souza & Nepal, *Smart Australians*.

30. The Australian Bureau of Statistics does not produce price indices for rural areas, making it impossible to precisely answer the question of whether the price differences are larger or smaller than the income differences. One way to consider the issue is to compare the cost of living across Australian cities, which yields a 7 per cent difference between the two most different cities, Adelaide and Sydney: B. Phillips, *NATSEM Household Budget Report: Cost of living and standard of living indexes for Australia, June quarter 2013*, Canberra: NATSEM, 2013, p. 21. Another is to use the 2011 Census to compare median weekly rent costs as a proportion of median (Australia-wide) income. This yields a difference of 28 per cent in Sydney ($350/$1234) versus 13 per cent in rural Queensland ($166/$1234), suggesting a 15 per cent cost of living differential.

31. C.E. Landry, J.A. List, M.K. Price & N.G. Rupp, 'Toward an Understanding of the Economics of Charity: Evidence from a field experiment', *Quarterly Journal of Economics*, 2006, vol. 121, no. 6, pp. 747–82; M. Belot, V. Bhaskar & J. van de Ven, 'Beauty and the Sources of Discrimination', *Journal of Human Resources*, 2012, vol. 47, pp. 851–72; N. Mocan & E. Tekin, 'Ugly Criminals', *Review of Economics and Statistics*, 2010, vol. 92, pp. 15–30; J.E. Stewart, 'Defendant's Attractiveness as a Factor in the Outcome of Criminal Trials: An Observational Study', *Journal of Applied Social Psychology*, 1980, vol. 10, no. 4, pp. 348–61; R. Mazzella & A. Feingold, 'The Effects of Physical Attractiveness, Race, Socioeconomic Status, and Gender of Defendants and Victims on Judgments of Mock Jurors: A Meta-analysis', *Journal of Applied Social Psychology*, 1994, vol. 24, no. 15, pp. 1315–38.

32. On employee share-ownership plans, see J.R. Blasi, D.L. Kruse & H.M. Markowitz, 'Risk and Lack of Diversification under Employee Ownership and Shared Capitalism', in *Shared Capitalism at Work: Employee ownership, profit and gain sharing, and broad-based stock options*, Chicago: University of Chicago Press, 2010, pp. 105–138; J.R. Blasi, R.B. Freeman, C. Mackin & D.L. Kruse, (2010), 'Creating a Bigger Pie? The effects of employee ownership, profit sharing, and stock options on workplace performance', in D.L. Kruse, R.B. Freeman & J.R. Blasi (eds), *Shared Capitalism at Work*, Chicago: University of Chicago Press, pp. 139–165. On union wage effects, see M. Wooden, 'Union Wage Effects in the Presence of Enterprise Bargaining', *Economic Record*, 2001, vol. 77, no. 236, pp. 1–18. On the wage penalty for gay men, see for example D.A. Black, H.R. Makar, S.G. Sanders & L.J. Taylor, 'The Earnings Effects of Sexual Orientation', *Industrial and Labor Relations Review*, 2003, vol. 56, no. 3, pp. 449–69. On racial discrimination in hiring, see A.L. Booth, A. Leigh & E. Varganova, 'Does Ethnic Discrimination Vary Across Minority Groups? Evidence from a field experiment', *Oxford Bulletin of Economics and Statistics*, 2012, vol. 74, no. 4, pp. 547–73.

Chapter 5: Careering through life

1. T.A. Salthouse, T.M. Atkinson & D.E. Berish. 'Executive Functioning as a Potential Mediator of Age-related Cognitive Decline in Normal Adults', *Journal of Experimental Psychology: General*, 2003, vol. 132, no. 4, p. 566; S. Agarwal, J.C. Driscoll, X. Gabaix & D. Laibson, *The Age of Reason: Financial decisions over the lifecycle*, National Bureau of Economic Research Working Paper no. 13191, Cambridge, MA: NBER, 2008.

2. Quoted in David Galenson, *Old Masters and Young Geniuses: The two life cycles of artistic creativity*, Princeton, NJ: Princeton University Press, 2006, p. 5.

3. Galenson, *Old Masters and Young Geniuses*, p. 22.

4. Quoted in Galenson, *Old Masters and Young Geniuses*, p. 147. If you think that's harsh, Martin Amis said in 2009 that old age was 'like starring in a low-budget horror film, saving the worst till last': quoted in Patrick Kidd, 'The Play's No Longer Quite the Same Thing for Stoppard', *The Australian*, 17 October 2013.

5. Quoted in Galenson, *Old Masters and Young Geniuses*, p. 126.

6. Galenson, *Old Masters and Young Geniuses*, p. 157.

7. The best ranking of Australian painters based on auction prices is set out in B. Coate, 'An Economic Analysis of the Auction Market for Australian Art: Evidence of Indigenous difference and creative achievement', PhD thesis, Melbourne: RMIT University, 2009. In Table 5.8 (model 2a), Coate ranked the top ten Australian artists as John Brack, Jeffrey Smart, Frederick McCubbin, Brett Whiteley, Tom Roberts, Ian Fairweather, Fred Williams, Margaret Preston, John Kelly and Russell Drysdale. This reflects the fact that the best works by earlier artists such as Streeton, Nolan and Boyd simply did not change hands during the period that Coate analyses. See also H. Higgs, 'Australian Art Market Prices During the Global Financial Crisis and Two Earlier Decades', *Australian Economic Papers*, 2012, vol. 51, no. 4, pp. 189–209.

8. The compendiums were S. Mellville & J. Rollinson, *Australian Art and Artists*, Sydney: Science Press, 1996; L. Hunter, *The Australian Art Companion: A selection of influential artists*, Sydney: Reed Books, 1990; and *Australian Art Masterpieces*, Melbourne: Viking O'Neil, 1987. For the purpose of selecting each artist's top artwork, I also consulted three other texts: R. Hughes, *The Art of Australia*, 2nd edn, Melbourne: Penguin, 1970; B. Smith, *Australian Painting 1788–2000*, South Melbourne: Oxford University Press, 2001; and J. Anderson (ed.), *The Cambridge Companion to Australian Art*, Cambridge: Cambridge University Press, 2011.

9. Quoted in Hughes, *The Art of Australia*, p. 54.

10. Hughes, *The Art of Australia*, p. 61; A. McCulloch & S. McCulloch, *The New McCulloch's Encyclopedia of Australian Art*, Sydney: Allen & Unwin, 1994.

11. Quoted in P. Haynes, *Sidney Nolan: Foundation Collection*, 2012, Canberra: Canberra Museum and Gallery, p.17.

12. R. Nelson, Review of Sidney Nolan at NGV Australia, *The Age*, 27 February 2008; M. Terry, 'Lambert, George Washington Thomas (1873–1930)', *Australian Dictionary of Biography*, <http://adb.anu.edu.au>, accessed 23 February 2014.

13. Robert Hughes, 'Arthur Boyd, Seeking the Wild', *Time Magazine*, vol. 143, no. 18, 2 May 1994.

14. Hughes, *The Art of Australia*, p. 184.

15. Hughes, *The Art of Australia*, pp. 191, 199.

16. N. Drury, 'The Spiritual Perspective of Aboriginal Painter Rover Thomas', *Nevill Drury*, <www.nevilldrury.com/nevill-drury-articles-rover-thomas.htm>, accessed 23 February 2014.

17. Sylvia Kleinert, 2000, 'Namatjira, Albert (Elea) (1902–1959)', *Australian Dictionary of Biography*, <http://adb.anu.edu.au>, accessed 23 February 2014.

18. Quoted in 'Utopia: The Genius of Emily Kame Kngwarreye', *National Museum of Australia*, <www.nma.gov.au/exhibitions/utopia_the_genius_of_emily_kame_kngwarreye/home>, accessed 23 February 2014.

19. The book is J. O'Donnell, T. Creswell & C. Mathieson, *100 Best Australian Albums*, Melbourne: Hardie Grant Books, 2010. The survey of 175 industry experts and Triple J listeners were both conducted by ABC Triple J in 2011, and the results are available at 'Hottest 100 Australian Albums of All Time', *ABC*, <www.abc.net.au/triplej/hottest100/alltime/11/>, accessed 23 February 2014. The lists were summed by assigning each rank a number of points (1st = 100 points and so on down to 100th = 1 point), and then summing the total number of points

for each band. Note that all three sources were male-dominated: the book is written by three men, the industry experts are more likely to be men, and surveys of Triple J listeners find that there are more men than women. I do not use album sales data in this analysis, but it is worth noting that a 2006 newspaper article listed the five best-selling Australian albums of all time as: John Farnham's *Whispering Jack* (1,680,000 Australian sales), Delta Goodrem's *Innocent Eyes* (980,000 sales) Savage Garden's self-titled album (840,000 sales), Crowded House's *Recurring Dream* (770,000 sales) and John Farnham's *Age Of Reason* (770,000 sales): 'How Farnham fought back', *Sunday Telegraph*, 3 December 2006. Another source puts total Australian sales of AC/DC's *Back in Black* at 840,000: ARIA, 'ARIA Charts—Accreditations—2013 Albums', 31 December 2013, <www.aria.com.au>, accessed 24 February 2014.

20. O'Donnell, Creswell & Mathieson, *100 Best Australian Albums*.

21. Quoted in O'Donnell, Creswell & Mathieson, *100 Best Australian Albums*.

22. Finn brothers quoted in O'Donnell, Creswell & Mathieson, *100 Best Australian Albums*, p. 27; Dylan quoted in Clinton Heylin, *Still on the Road: The songs of Bob Dylan, 1974–2006*, Chicago: Chicago Review Press, 2010, p. 445. I am grateful to David Galenson for drawing this quote to my attention.

23. Quoted in A. Bennie (ed.), *Crème de la Phlegm: Unforgettable Australian reviews*, Melbourne: The Miegunyah Press, 2006, p. 193.

24. Quoted in O'Donnell, Creswell & Mathieson, *100 Best Australian Albums*, p. 17.

25. Quoted in O'Donnell, Creswell & Mathieson, *100 Best Australian Albums*, p. 28.

26. Published in S. Reynolds, *Blissed Out: The raptures of rock*, London: Serpent's Tail, 1990, p.75.

27. B. Zuel, 'At 55, Nick Cave Finally Becomes a Chart-topper in His Homeland', *Sydney Morning Herald*, 27 February 2013.

28. The First Tuesday list contained 10 books, and was compiled in 2012, '10 Aussie Books to Read Before You Die', ABC, <www.abc.net.au/arts/aussiebooks/>, accessed 23 February 2014. The Australian Society of Authors list contained 40 books, and was reported in Catherine Keenan, 'Authors' Top Reads', *Sydney Morning Herald*, 27 May 2003. The Booktopia list of '50 Must Read Australian Novels' was based on a 2011 poll, and was available at <www.blog.booktopia.com.au> (the list included no more than one book per author). The lists were combined by assigning each rank a number of points (1st = 100 points and so on down to 50th = 50 points), and then summing the total number of points for each author.

29. 'Markus Zusak talks about the writing of *The Book Thief*', Pan Macmillan, 2007, <www.panmacmillan.com.au>, accessed 24 February 2014.

30. As Zusak describes the book's theme, 'Then came an idea that I'd had floating in my head for a couple of years about a stealer of books. Soon I realised that words were a good metaphor for Nazi Germany. It was words (and Hitler's ability to use them) that contained the power to murder and ostracise. What I set out to create was a character to juxtapose the way Hitler used words. She would be a stealer of books and a prolific reader.': 'Markus Zusak talks about the writing of *The Book Thief*', Pan Macmillan, 2007, <www.panmacmillan.com.au>, accessed 24 February 2014.

31. J. Franzen, 'Rereading "The Man Who Loved Children"', *New York Times*, 3 June 2010.

32. M. Harris, 'Stead, Christina Ellen (1902–1983)', *Australian Dictionary of Biography*, <http://adb.anu.edu.au>, accessed 23 February 2014.

33. T. Gilling, 'INSPIRE: David Malouf', Weekend Magazine, *The Australian*, 2 August 2008.

34. D. Marr, 'Patrick White: The final chapter', *The Monthly*, no. 33, April 2008.

35. J. Hooton, *Ruth Park: A celebration*, Canberra: Friends of the National Library of Australia, 1996, p. 8; R. Park, *Fishing in the Styx*, Melbourne: Viking, 1993, pp. 65, 222.

36. Interview with R. Koval on *The Book Show*, ABC radio, 1 October 2008.

37. Both quotes from K. Grenville interview with S. Errington, 2008, <www.kategrenville.com/node/71>, accessed 23 February 2014.

38. T. O'Neill, 'Lindsay, Joan á Beckett (1896–1984)', *Australian Dictionary of Biography*, <http://adb.anu.edu.au>, accessed 23 February 2014.

39. 'Norman Lindsay Biography', *Norman Lindsay: Australia's most iconic and controversial artist*, <www.normanlindsay.net/about-norman-lindsay/72-norman-lindsay-biography>, accessed 23 February 2014; B. Smith, 'Lindsay, Norman Alfred (1879–1969)', *Australian Dictionary of Biography*, <http://adb.anu.edu.au>, accessed 23 February 2014.

40. Both quotes from J. Steger, 'The Sea Side of Tim Winton', *The Age*, 26 April 2008.

41. Both quotes from P. Daley, 'Dirt Smart', *The Age*, 29 May 2002.

42. B. Jones, E.J. Reedy and B.A. Weinberg, 'Age and Scientific Genius', 2014, NBER Working Paper no. 19866, Cambridge, MA: National Bureau of Economic Research.

Chapter 6: Cops and dollars

1. This account of the Hoddle Street massacre draws on P. Haddow, *Hoddle Street: The Ambush and the Tragedy*, Melbourne: Strategic Australia, 1987. Other accounts include Anon., *Julian Knight—the Hoddle Street Massacre*, <www.julianknight-hoddlestreet.ca/julian-knight-research-file/hoddle-street-massacre.html>, accessed 24 February 2014 and 'Time Capsule—August 9, 1987: Seven killed, 19 injured in Hoddle Street massacre', *The Weekend Australian Magazine*, 4 August 2007.

2. M.L. Fackler, *Wound Ballistics Research of the Past Twenty Years: A giant step backwards*, Institute Report no. 447, San Francisco: Letterman Army Institute of Research, 1990.

3. This account of the Port Arthur massacre draws on M. Bingham, *Suddenly One Sunday*, Sydney: HarperCollins, 1996, and M. Scott, 1997, *Port Arthur: A story of strength and courage*, Sydney: Random House, 1997.

4. P. Reuter & J. Mouzos, 'Australia: A massive buyback of low-risk guns' in J. Ludwig & P.J. Cook (eds), *Evaluating Gun Policy: Effects on Crime and Violence*, Washington, DC: Brookings Institution Press, 2003, pp. 121–56; A. Leigh & C. Neill, 'Do Gun Buybacks Save Lives? Evidence from panel data', *American Law and Economics Review*, 2010, vol. 12, no. 2, pp. 462–508.

5. S. Chapman, P. Alpers, K. Agho & M. Jones, 'Australia's 1996 Gun Law Reforms: Faster falls in firearm deaths, firearm suicides, and a decade without mass shootings', *Injury Prevention*, 2006, vol. 12, pp. 365–72.

6. C. Neill & A. Leigh, 'Do Gun Buybacks Save Lives? Evidence from time series variation', *Current Issues in Criminal Justice*, 2008, vol. 20, no. 2, pp. 145–62.

7. The Bureau of Meteorology estimates that five to ten Australians are killed by lightning strikes each year. 'Severe Thunderstorms', *Bureau of Meteorology*, <www.bom.gov.au/info/thunder/#protection>, accessed 24 February 2014. For earlier years, see also L. Coates, R. Blong and F. Siciliano, 'Lightning fatalities in Australia, 1824–1991', *Natural Hazards*, vol. 8, pp. 217–33.

8. Leigh & Neill, 'Do Gun Buybacks Save Lives?'.

9. P. Abelson, 'The Value of Life and Health for Public Policy', *Economic Record*, 2003, vol. 79, pp. S2–S13.

10. The 1996 road toll was 1970 people: Australian Transport Safety Bureau, *Road Deaths Australia 2006 Statistical Summary*, Canberra: Australian Transport Safety Bureau, Table 30.

11. P. Grabosky, *Fear of Crime and Fear Reduction Strategies, Trends and Issues in Crime and Criminal Justice*, report no. 44, Canberra: Australian Institute of Criminology, 1995. See also B. Davis & K. Dossetor, *(Mis)perceptions of Crime in Australia*, Trends and Issues in Crime and Criminal Justice, report no. 396, Canberra: Australian Institute of Criminology, 2010.

12. F. Cornaglia, N. Feldman & A. Leigh, 2014, 'Crime and Mental Well-Being', *Journal of Human Resources*, vol. 49, no. 2, pp. 110–40.

13. J.J. Donohue III & S.D. Levitt, 'The Impact of Legalized Abortion on Crime', *Quarterly Journal of Economics*, 2001, vol. 116, no. 2, pp. 379–420.

14. A. Leigh & J. Wolfers, 'Abortion and Crime', *AQ: Journal of Contemporary Analysis*, 2000, vol. 72, no. 4, pp. 28–30 (originally published in op-ed form as A. Leigh & J. Wolfers, 'Abortion's Secret Legacy', *The Age*, 11 November 1999).

15. On the (modest) relationship between total fertility and legalised abortion, see for example J. Klerman, 'U.S. Abortion Policy and Fertility', Santa Monica, CA: RAND Corporation, RB–5031, 2000, <www.rand.org/pubs/research_briefs/RB5031>, accessed 24 February 2014.

16. S. Levitt & S. Dubner, *Freakonomics*, New York: HarperCollins, 2005, p. 144.

17. J.W. Reyes, 'Environmental Policy as Social Policy? The impact of childhood lead exposure on crime', *B.E. Journal of Economic Analysis & Policy*, 2007, vol. 7, no. 1.

18. L. O'Dwyer, 'Using GIS to Identify Risk of Elevated Blood Lead Levels in Children in Adelaide', *Australian Geographical Studies*, 2001, vol. 39, pp. 75–90.

19. S.D. Levitt, 'Understanding Why Crime Fell in the 1990s: Four factors that explain the decline and six that do not', *Journal of Economic Perspectives*, 2004, vol. 18, no. 1, pp. 163–90. The number of police officers per 100,000 Australians was 170 in 1970, 215 in 1980, 230 in 1990, 222 in

2000 and 240 in 2011. Using Levitt's estimate of the relationship between police numbers and crime rates, the 27 per cent increase from 1970 to 1980 would account for an 11 per cent drop in crime in the 1970s, but the changes in police numbers since 1980 are too small to have had a substantial effect on crime rates.

20. Levitt, 'Understanding Why Crime Fell in the 1990s'. See also A. Barbarino and G. Mastrobuoni, 'The Incapacitation Effect of Incarceration: Evidence from Several Italian Collective Pardons', *American Economic Journal: Economic Policy*, 2014, vol. 6, no. 1, pp. 1–37.

21. The 1991 figures from A. Leigh, 'Reducing Crime and Incarceration', House of Representatives Hansard, 21 November 2011. The 2013 figures are from Australian Bureau of Statistics, *Prisoners in Australia, 2013*, Canberra: ABS; costs from Productivity Commission, *Report on Government Services 2010*, Canberra: Productivity Commission, 2011.

22. Australian Bureau of Statistics, *Prisoners in Australia, 2013*, Cat. no. 4517.0, Canberra: ABS, 2013.

23. Australian Bureau of Statistics, *National Aboriginal and Torres Strait Islander Social Survey 2008*, Cat. no. 4714.0, Canberra: ABS, 2009.

24. On the drop in crime during the noughties, see Australian Institute of Criminology *Australian Crime: Facts & figures: 2011*, Canberra: Australian Institute of Criminology, 2012.

25. On this issue, see S.N. Durlauf & D.S. Nagin, 'Imprisonment and Crime: Can both be reduced?', *Criminology & Public Policy*, 2011, vol. 10, no. 1, pp. 13–54 and M.A.R. Kleiman, *When Brute Force Fails: How to have less crime and less punishment*, Princeton, NJ: Princeton University Press, 2009.

26. Bruce Western, 'Testimony Before the Joint Economic Committee' in Joint Economic Committee, 'Mass Incarceration in the United States: At What Cost?' Hearing before the Joint Economic Committee, Congress of the United States 110th Congress, First Session, 4 October 2007, Washington DC: US Government Printing Office, 2008, pp. 15–17.

27. Heilpern, D., *Fear or Favour: Sexual Assault of Young Prisoners*, Lismore: Southern Cross University Press, 1998.

28. On the intergenerational crime correlation, see V. Goodwin & B. Davis, *Crime Families: Gender and the intergenerational transfer of criminal tendencies*, Trends and Issues in Crime and Criminal Justice, report no. 414, Canberra: Australian Institute of Criminology, 2011. As to working with children of prisoners, one of my favourite such organisations is 'SHINE for Kids'.

29. M. Gatto & T. Noble, *I, Mick Gatto*, Melbourne: Victory Books, 2010.

30. S. Dawe (ed.), *Vocational education and training for adult prisoners and offenders in Australia: Research readings*, Adelaide: NCVER, 2007.

31. This is despite the fact that, according to the Productivity Commission's annual *Report on Government Services*, states and territories have formally agreed to 'Provide program interventions to reduce the risk of re-offending'.

32. Some measure of the extreme disadvantage among the Perry Preschool population can be gleaned from the fact that the average person in the control group had 4.6 arrests (including 1.5 felony arrests) by age 27. By contrast, the treatment group had 'only' 2.3 arrests (including 0.7 felony arrests) by the same age: D.J. Besharov, P. Germanis, C.A. Higney & D.M. Call, 'The High/Scope Perry Preschool Project', in *Assessments of Twenty-Six Early Childhood Evaluations*, College Park, MD: University of Maryland School of Public Policy Welfare Reform Academy, 2011, ch. 16. The randomised experiment on school quality is reported in D. Deming, 'Better Schools, Less Crime?', *Quarterly Journal of Economics*, 2011, vol. 126, no. 4, pp. 2063–115.

33. S. Aos, M. Miller & E. Drake, *Evidence-based Public Policy Options to Reduce Future Prison Construction, Criminal Justice Costs, and Crime Rates*, Olympia, Washington: Washington State Institute for Public Policy, 2006.

34. See for example Kleiman, *When Brute Force Fails*.

35. L.W. Sherman, H. Strang, C. Angel, D. Woods, G.C. Barnes, S.Bennett & N. Inkpen, 'Effects of Face-to-Face Restorative Justice on Victims of Crime in Four Randomized, Controlled Trials', *Journal of Experimental Criminology*, 2005, vol. 1, no. 3, pp. 367–95; J. Braithwaite, *Restorative Justice and Responsive Regulation*, Oxford: Oxford University Press, 2002. H. Strang, L.W. Sherman, E. Mayo-Wilson, D. Woods, and B. Ariel, 'Restorative Justice Conferencing (RJC) Using Face-to-Face Meetings of Offenders and Victims: Effects on Offender Recidivism and Victim Satisfaction. A Systematic Review', *Campbell Systematic Reviews*, vol. 9, issue 12, 2013.

36. See also M. Duncan, A. Leigh, D. Madden & P. Tynan, *Imagining Australia: Ideas for Our Future*, Sydney: Allen & Unwin, 2004; M. Kleiman, 'Stop the Revolving Door', *Blueprint Magazine*, 25 September 2002. I am grateful to Justin Wolfers for valuable discussions on this point.

37. Coutts-Trotter's story is set out in A. Summers, 2012, 'Cool, calm, elected', *Sydney Morning Herald*, 22 September 2012.

38. 'O'Farrell Puts Stamp on Public Service', *The Australian*, 1 April 2011.

Chapter 7: Helping the world's poor

1. I heard Jaqueline Lima speak at the Global Fund 4th Partnership Forum in São Paulo, Brazil, on 28 June 2011. A version of her life story can be found online: 'Jacqueline Lima's story of courage and success', *The Global Fund to fight AIDS, Tuberculosis and Malaria*, <www.theglobal fund.org/en/partnershipforum/2011/speeches/>, accessed 24 February 2014.

2. J. Sachs, *The End of Poverty: Economic possibilities for our time*, New York: Penguin Books, 2005.

3. W. Easterly, *The Elusive Quest for Growth: Economists' adventures and misadventures in the tropics*, Cambridge, MA: MIT Press, 2001; W. Easterly, *The White Man's Burden: Why the West's efforts to aid the rest have done so much ill and so little good*, New York: Penguin Books, 2006.

4. C. Burnside & D. Dollar, 'Aid, Policies, and Growth', *American Economic Review*, 2000, vol. 90, no. 4, pp. 847–68; W. Easterly, R. Levine & D. Roodman, 'Aid, Policies, and Growth: Comment', *American Economic Review*, 2004, vol. 94, no. 3, pp. 774–80; P. Collier & D. Dollar, 'Can the World Cut Poverty in Half? How policy reform and effective aid can meet international development goals', 2001, *World Development*, vol. 29, no. 11, pp. 1787–802.

5. R. Fisman & E. Miguel, 'Corruption, Norms and Legal Enforcement: Evidence from diplomatic parking tickets', *Journal of Political Economy*, 2007, vol. 115, no. 6, pp. 1020–48. Their study focused on the period before a major crackdown in 2002, when New York City finally refused to re-register cars with unpaid parking fines.

6. Australia's top nine aid recipients all score in the bottom half of Transparency International's 2011 corruption ranking.

7. P. Collier, *The Plundered Planet: Why we must—and how we can— manage nature for global prosperity*, Oxford: Oxford University Press, 2010.

8. In 2009–10, AusAID's losses to fraud were just 0.028 per cent of the total aid program. Centrelink's proportional loss to fraud is considerably higher. Fraud losses for businesses operating in Australia are estimated by KPMG, *Fraud and Misconduct Survey 2010*, Sydney: KPMG, 2010, <http://www.kpmg.com>, accessed 19 March 2014. A 2009 Australian National Audit Office report stated: 'AusAID's cautious approach to fund provision, while minimising the risk of corruption, has sometimes prevented resources getting to where they are most needed'. See ANAO, *AusAID's Management of the Expanding Australian Aid Program*, ANAO Audit Report No.15 2009–10, Canberra: ANAO, 2009.

9. On the shortcomings of China's aid program, see e.g. F. Hanson and M. Fifita, 'China in the Pacific: the new banker in town', 2011, Lowy Institute Policy Brief, Sydney: Lowy Institute.

10. UK Department for International Development, 'Case Study:

Technology to tackle corruption', *Department for International Development*, <https://www.dfid.gov.uk/stories/case-studies/2010/technology-to-tackle-corruption/>, accessed 24 February 2014.

11. PEW Research Centre, *Global Attitudes Project*, available at <www.pew global.org>, accessed 24 February 2014. The question (asked only of Muslims) was 'Some people think that suicide bombing and other forms of violence against civilian targets are justified in order to defend Islam from its enemies. Other people believe that, no matter what the reason, this kind of violence is never justified. Do you personally feel that this kind of violence is often justified to defend Islam, sometimes justified, rarely justified, or never justified?' I report the proportion of Muslims who answered 'often justified' or 'sometimes justified'. In most countries, this figure has fallen over the past decade. National Consortium for the Study of Terrorism and Responses to Terrorism (START) (*Global Terrorism Database* [data file]), <http://www.start.umd.edu/gtd>, accessed 24 February 2014.

12. A.B. Krueger, *What Makes a Terrorist: Economics and the roots of terrorism*, Princeton, NJ: Princeton University Press, 2007.

13. This section draws heavily on E. Berman, *Radical, Religious and Violent: The new economics of terrorism*, Cambridge, MA: MIT Press, 2009.

14. D. Kilcullen, *The Accidental Guerrilla: Fighting small wars in the midst of a big one*, Oxford: Oxford University Press, 2009.

15. Collier, *The Plundered Planet*.

16. Collier's estimate is US$114,000. At the time of writing, the USD and AUD were close to parity.

17. See *Natural Resource Charter*, <www.naturalresourcecharter.org>, accessed 24 February 2014.

18. Some of this knowledge is currently being conveyed through the Australian Centre for International Agricultural Research, and our involvement in the World Food Programme and the G20's Committee for World Food Security.

19. G. Mills, *Why Africa is Poor: And what Africans can do about it*, New York: Penguin Global, 2010, pp. 136, 141. On extending Malawi's success, see for example J.W. McArthur, *An International Credit Facility To Support Commercialization of African Smallholder Staple Crop Farmers*, Concept Note for GAC on Poverty and Economic Development, New York: Millennium Promise Alliance, 2011.

20. E. Miguel, *Africa's Turn?*, Cambridge MA: MIT Press, 2009, p. 40.

21. See for example Miguel, *Africa's Turn?*.

22. The top five recipients of Australian aid in 2013-14 were projected to be Indonesia, Papua New Guinea, Solomon Islands, Afghanistan and Vietnam: B. Carr, *Australia's International Development Assistance Program, Budget 2013–14, Ministerial Statement*, 14 May 2013, Canberra: AusAID, p. 12.

23. R. Guest, *The Shackled Continent: Power, corruption, and African lives*, Washington, DC: Smithsonian Books, 2004.

24. M. Fullilove, *The Testament of Solomons: RAMSI and international state-building*, Sydney: Lowy Institute Analysis, 2006.

25. This story is told in C. Wattegama 'Nobody told us to run' in N. Gunawardene & F. Noronha (eds), *Communicating Disasters: An Asia Pacific resource book*, Bangkok: UNDP Regional Centre, 2007, pp. 21–6.

26. S. Feeny & M. Clarke, 'What Determines Australia's Response to Natural Disasters?', *Australian Economic Review*, 2007, vol. 40, no. 1, pp. 24–36. Feeny and Clarke found that a 10 per cent increase in the number of articles was associated with a 10 per cent increase in the amount of money given by private donors to World Vision, and with a 37 per cent increase in the resources provided via AusAID's emergency relief scheme.

27. T. Eisensee & D. Strömberg, 'News Droughts, News Floods, and U.S. Disaster Relief', *Quarterly Journal of Economics*, 2007, vol. 122, no. 2, pp. 693–728.

28. M. Faye & P. Niehaus, 'Political aid cycles', *American Economic Review*, 2012, vol. 102, no. 7, pp. 3516–30; I. Kuziemko & E. Werker, 'How Much

Is a Seat on the Security Council Worth? Foreign aid and bribery at
the United Nations', *Journal of Political Economy*, 2006, vol. 114, no. 5,
pp. 905–30.

Chapter 8: Smashing the crystal ball

1. There is some disagreement between Keen and Robertson over the
   precise terms of the bet. See M. Janda, 2010, 'Economist Keen to walk
   Canberra–Kosciuszko', ABC News, 16 February 2010; Steve Keen,
   'A Monkey Off My Back', 12 May 2010, <www.debtdeflation.com>,
   accessed 24 February 2014.
2. An extensive investigation of the origins of this quote concluded that
   it was first uttered by an unknown author in Danish before 1948. See
   G. O'Toole, 2013, 'It's Difficult to Make Predictions, Especially About the
   Future', 20 October 2013, <http://quoteinvestigator.com/2013/10/20/
   no-predict/>, accessed 24 February 2014.
3. Train travel quote from S. Smiles, *The Life of George Stephenson*, Jerusa-
   lem: Minerva Group, 2001, p. 93; Marconi quote from G. Weightman,
   *Signor Marconi's Magic Box: The Most Remarkable Invention of the 19th
   Century and the Amateur Inventor Whose Genius Sparked a Revolu-
   tion*, Cambridge, MA: Da Capo Press, 2009, ch. 41; Ballmer quote from
   D. Lieberman, 'CEO Forum: Microsoft's Ballmer having a "great time"',
   USA Today, 30 April 2007.
4. M. Obel, 'Economic Indicator: Look inside the cardboard box', *Tampa
   Bay Times*, 7 April 2009; Y. Q. Mui, 'Blue Chip, White Cotton: What
   underwear says about the economy', *Washington Post*, 31 August 2009.
5. M. van Baardwijk & Ph. H.B.F. Franses, *The Hemline and the Economy:
   Is there any match?*, Working Paper no. EI 2010–40, Rotterdam: Erasmus
   University Econometric Institute, 2010. T.F. Pettijohn & D.F. Sacco,
   'Tough Times, Meaningful Music, Mature Performers: Popular Bill-
   board songs and performer preferences across social and economic

conditions in the USA', *Psychology of Music*, 2009, vol. 37, no. 2, pp. 155–79. A variant of this is the finding that 'beat volatility' within top songs is associated with US share market volatility the subsequent year: P. Maymin, 'Music and the Market: Song and stock volatility', *North American Journal of Economics and Finance*, 2012, vol. 23, no. 1, pp. 70–85. See also P. Maymin, 'Flop Culture', *New York Post*, 1 February 2009. T.F. Pettijohn & B.J. Jungeberg, 'Playboy Playmate Curves: Changes in facial and body feature preferences across social and economic conditions', *Personality and Social Psychology Bulletin*, 2004, vol. 30, no. 9, pp. 1186–97. See also N. Barber, 'The Slender Ideal and Eating Disorders: An interdisciplinary "telescope" model', *International Journal of Eating Disorders*, 1998, vol. 23, no. 3, pp. 295–307.

6. The growth rate in 1998–99 was 5.3 per cent. *Age* newspaper quote from 2007 from B. Schneiders & N. Khadem, 'Looking Good', *The Age*, 30 June 2007, p. 1. Forecasts for growth in calendar year 2008 ranged from 2.5 to 4.5 per cent. The growth rate was 1.9 per cent. V. O'Shaughnessy, 'Forecasts Were Way Out for 2008', *The Age*, 3 January 2009, p. 11.

7. G. Stevens, 'Better than a Coin Toss? The Thankless Task of Economic Forecasting', *Reserve Bank of Australia Bulletin*, September 2004, pp. 6–14 (Stevens acknowledges the assistance of Jonathan Kearns in preparing the analysis).

8. P. Tulip & S. Wallace, *Estimates of Uncertainty Around the RBA's Forecasts*, Reserve Bank Discussion Paper RDP 2012-07, Sydney: RBA, 2012, p. 11.

9. D. Chessell, P. Crone, M. Edey & L. Williams, *Review of Treasury Macroeconomic and Revenue Forecasting*, Canberra: Australian Treasury, 2012, p. 35.

10. D. Gruen, 'Forecasting Methods: Final observations—economic forecasters aren't stupid; what we are trying to do is hard!', in P. Abelson & R. Joyeux, (eds), *Economic Forecasting*, Sydney: Allen & Unwin, 2000.

11. W. Swan, 'Australia to 2050: future challenges', *Intergenerational Report*

2010, Canberra: Australian Treasury, 2010, pp. 159, 160. The 2002 *Intergenerational Report* forecast a population of 24.5 million in 2035 and 25.3 million in 2042: P. Costello, *Intergenerational Report 2002–03*, 2002–03 Budget Paper no. 5, Canberra: Australian Treasury, 2002, p. 22. Extrapolating forward, this implies a population around 26 million in 2047.

12. The report is Department of Employment, Education and Training, *Australia's Workforce 2005: Jobs in the Future*, Canberra: Australian Government, 1995. The estimates covered the period 1994–2005, and are presented as the middle scenario ('Scenario II') in Table A3.1. I use industry estimates because occupational codes changed over this period. The actual change compares average industry employment in the four quarters of 1994 with average industry employment in the four quarters of 2005. Regressing actual results on forecasts returns an R-squared of 0.002. In 2011, the Centre of Policy Studies evaluated the accuracy of their own labour market forecasts, produced using the MONASH Forecasting Model. Analysing predictions eight years out, the study found average errors of 9 per cent when using 18 industries, and 16–20 per cent or more when forecasting at a finer level (such as hundreds of occupations or industries). The report noted that a linear trend extrapolation had larger forecast errors. See G. Meagher & F. Pang, *Labour Market Forecasting, Reliability and Workforce Development*, General Paper no. G-225, Melbourne: Centre of Policy Studies, Monash University, 2011, pp. 11–14.

13. P.D. Adams & G. Meagher, *Australia's Workforce Trends to 2010: Forecasts from the MONASH model*, Melbourne: Centre of Policy Studies, Monash University 1999. B. Jones, 'The Knowledge Nation Task Force: Transformation in Australia', AUSTAFE Conference, Alice Springs, 2001. Mining's share of gross value-added was around 5 per cent in 2001, and around 10 per cent in 2011: M. Parkinson, 'Challenges and Opportunities for the Australian Economy', speech to the John Curtin Institute of Public Policy, Breakfast Forum, Perth, 5 October 2012.

14. R.B. Freeman, *Is A Great Labor Shortage Coming? Replacement demand in the global economy*, NBER Working Paper no. 12541, Cambridge, MA: National Bureau of Economic Research, 2006.

15. B.G. Malkiel, *A Random Walk Down Wall Street: The Time-tested Strategy for Successful Investing*, New York: W.W. Norton, 2007, p. 24.

16. Mercer, 'Mercer Investment Surveys—December 2012', 2013; J. Collett, 'Perpetual Ethical Fund Tops Performance as Share Funds Rebound', *Sydney Morning Herald*, 16 January 2013. See also A. Frino & D.R. Gallagher, 'Is Index Performance Achievable? An analysis of Australian equity index funds', *Abacus*, 2002, vol. 38, no. 2, pp. 200–14; 'Investment Returns: How active fund managers lost their lustre', Knowledge@ Australian School of Business, 24 August 2010, <http://knowledge.asb. unsw.edu.au>, accessed 24 February 2014. C. Becker, 'Troubles with Fund Management—An absolute return view', *MacroBusiness Blog*, 6 April 2011, <www.macrobusiness.com.au/2011/04/troubles-with-fund-management-absolute-returnr/>, accessed 24 February 2014.

17. 'R & D Funding in Australia', *The Science Show*, ABC radio, broadcast 2 September 2000.

18. M. Crosby, 'Exchange Rate Forecasts', *Core Economics Blog*, 10 March 2009, <http://economics.com.au/?p=2879>, accessed 24 February 2014. Historical exchange rates from <www.oanda.com/currency/historical-rates/>, accessed 24 February 2014. AAP, 'Money Guru Predicts Aussie Dollar Will Hit $1.70 by 2014', *NineMSN Finance*, 9 May 2011, <http:// finance.ninemsn.com.au>, accessed 24 February 2014. <http://finance. ninemsn.com.au/newsbusiness/aap/8246595/money-guru-predicts-aussie-dollar-will-hit-1-70-by-2014>.

19. N. Silver, *The Signal and the Noise: Why so many predictions fail—but some don't*, New York: Penguin, 2012; Commonwealth Bureau of Meteorology, *Submission to the House of Representatives Select Committee on the Recent Australian Bushfires*, Canberra: Parliament of Australia, 2003, pp. 31–2.

20. The excuses of erroneous forecasters are helpfully classified in P. Tetlock,

Expert Political Judgment: How good is it? How can we know? Princeton, NJ: Princeton University Press, 2005, p. 135.

21. Quoted in R. Hanson, 'Insider trading and prediction markets', *Journal of Law, Economics and Policy*, 2008, vol. 4, pp. 449–464 at p. 455 (I have omitted the Harvard-style references from the quotation).

22. R. Gurkaynak & J. Wolfers, 'Macroeconomic Derivatives: an initial analysis of market-based macro forecasts, uncertainty, and risk', in J.A. Frankel, & C.A. Pissarides (eds), *NBER International Seminar on Macroeconomics 2005*, NBER International Seminar on Macroeconomics Series, Cambridge, MA: MIT Press, 2007; P.M. Polgreen, F.D. Nelson, G.R. Neumann & R.A. Weinstein, 'Use of Prediction Markets to Forecast Infectious Disease Activity', *Clinical Infectious Diseases*, 2007, vol. 44, no. 2, pp. 272–9.

23. The tipping competition focused on rounds 1 to 23 of the 2012 AFL competition. Using the betting market favourite correctly predicted the results in 153 out of 198 games (77 per cent). This approach ranked me 36th out of 246 tipsters (and, I can't resist mentioning, ahead of the other six parliamentarians in the competition). Using a similar approach, my co-worker Thomas McMahon tells me that he won equal first place in his workplace's 2013 AFL tipping competition.

24. One study found that the average expert tipster for the *Age* and *Herald Sun* correctly forecast 65 per cent of matches: M. Amor & W. Griffiths, *Modelling the Behaviour and Performance of Australian Football Tipsters*, University of Melbourne Faculty of Economics Working Paper 03–871, Melbourne: University of Melbourne, 2003. Expert forecaster Greg Breen predicted only 75 per cent of the results in the first 23 rounds of the 2012 season: see www.footyforecaster.com.

25. S. Easton & K. Uylangco, 'Forecasting Outcomes in Tennis Matches Using Within-match Betting Markets', *International Journal of Forecasting*, 2010, vol. 26, no. 3, pp. 564–75.

26. See J. Wolfers & E. Zitzewitz, 'Prediction Markets', *Journal of Economic Perspectives*, 2004, vol. 18, no. 2, pp. 107–26.

27. I.D. Dichev, 'What Are Stock Investors' Actual Historical Returns? Evidence from dollar-weighted returns', *American Economic Review*, 2007, vol. 97, no. 1, pp. 386–401.

28. P. Gerrans, 'Retirement Savings Investment Choices in Response to the Global Financial Crisis: Australian evidence', *Australian Journal of Management*, 2012, vol. 37, no. 3, pp. 415–39.

29. The Australian Influenza Report is prepared by the Department of Health. The official unemployment, inflation and growth statistics are prepared by the Australian Bureau of Statistics.

30. F. Liu, B. Lv, G. Peng & X. Li, 'Influenza Epidemics Detection Based on Google Search Queries', in *Recent Progress in Data Engineering and Internet Technology*, Berlin: Springer, 2012, pp. 371–6; H. Choi & H. Varian, 'Predicting the Present with Google Trends', *Economic Record*, 2012, vol. 88, no. s1, pp. 2–9; N. McLaren & R. Shanbhogue, 'Using Internet Search Data as Economic Indicators', *Bank of England Quarterly Bulletin*, 2011-Q2, pp.134–40.

31. Hyunyoung Choi & Hal Varian, 2011, 'Predicting the Present with Google Trends', PowerPoint presentation to the San Francisco Federal Reserve, 18 March 2011.

32. O. Ashenfelter, D. Ashmore & R. Lalonde, 'Bordeaux Wine Vintage Quality and the Weather', *Chance*, 1995, vol. 8, no. 4, pp. 7–14. See also O. Ashenfelter, 'Predicting the Quality and Prices of Bordeaux Wine', *The Economic Journal*, 2008, vol. 118, no. 529, pp. F174–F184.

33. Interview with Kym Anderson, Adelaide, 16 October 2013.

34. R.P. Byron & O. Ashenfelter, 'Predicting the Quality of an Unborn Grange', *Economic Record*, 1995, vol. 71, no. 1, pp. 40–53; D. Wood & K. Anderson, 'What Determines the Future Value of an Icon Wine? New evidence from Australia', *Journal of Wine Economics*, 2006, vol. 1, no. 2, pp. 141–61.

35. Specifically, 'Penfold's Grange Hermitage is a blend of Shiraz grapes, drawn predominantly from the Barossa Valley but with contributions from Clare, McLaren Vale, the Magill vineyard near Adelaide

and, more recently, Coonawarra': Byron & Ashenfelter, 'Predicting the Quality of an Unborn Grange'. On the source of Grange grapes, see also A. Calliard, *Penfolds: The rewards of patience*, Sydney: Allen & Unwin, 2008.

36. My analysis follows Byron & Ashenfelter's paper, in that I use only the vintages from 1959 onwards, and obtain weather data for the same weather stations as they did.

37. To be precise, I estimate the following model: Log(Price) = –50.823 + 0.035 (Wine age)–0.00379 (Jan to Feb rainfall) + 5.826 (Oct to March temperature)–0.146 (Oct to March temperature squared)–0.225 (Oct to March temperature variation). For precise details of how the weather variables are defined, see Byron & Ashenfelter's, 'Predicting the Quality of an Unborn Grange'.

38. Langton's, 'Vintage Reports—Penfolds Grange', <www.langtons.com.au>, accessed 24 February 2014.

39. Across the 18 common observations, the correlation between the two ranking measures is –0.12.

40. Langton's, 'Vintage Reports'.

41. A. Leigh & R.D. Atkinson, *Clear Thinking on the Digital Divide*, Policy Report, Washington, DC: Progressive Policy Institute, 2001, p. 6; Thom File, 'Computer and Internet Use in the United States', P20–569, 2013, *United States Census Bureau*, <www.census.gov>, accessed 24 February 2014.

42. S. Dubner, 'The Folly of Prediction', *Freakonomics Radio*, broadcast 14 September 2011.

43. I. Berlin, *The Hedgehog and the Fox: An essay on Tolstoy's view of history*, New York: Simon & Schuster, 1953.

Chapter 9: Playing the blue guitar

1. C. Wright, *The Forgotten Rebels of Eureka*, Melbourne: Text Publishing, 2013, pp. 6, 165, 107.

2. Wright, *The Forgotten Rebels of Eureka*, p.165.

3. The alternative way of teaching economics is to teach the big principles once, then move on to the exceptions and extensions. Alas, it turns out that when you do this, many students remember virtually nothing about economics a year later. Two books that were influential in shaping my thinking on how to teach introductory economics were R.H. Frank, *The Economic Naturalist: Why economics explains almost everything*, New York: Random House, 2008, and B. Caplan, *The Myth of the Rational Voter: Why democracies choose bad policies*, Princeton. NJ: Princeton University Press, 2008.

4. A. Cornell & J. Stensholt, 'The Obsessions of Marius Kloppers (more than just soup)', *Australian Financial Review*, 14 July 2012.

5. 'How a Clean-FREAK Memo Derailed BHP boss', <News.com.au>, accessed 21 February 2013. On productivity and cleanliness, see M. Robin, 'Inside BHP Billiton's 11-page Office Rulebook: Do clean desks really boost productivity?', <SmartCompany.com.au>, accessed 10 July 2012.

6. In New South Wales, 19.5 per cent of kindergarten children are now held back a year, up from 17.3 per cent a decade ago: statistics quoted in C. Marriner, 2013, 'Delayed Start not Always a Good Idea', *Sun Herald*, 27 January 2013. For a review of the evidence on the effects of school starting age, see M. Konnikova, 'Youngest Kid, Smartest Kid?', *New Yorker*, 19 September 2013.

7. Quoted in S. Dubner, 'The Upside of Quitting', *Freakonomics Radio*, Season 1, Episode 5, 30 September 2011.

8. T. Cowen, *Discover Your Inner Economist: Use incentives to fall in love, survive your next meeting, and motivate your dentist*, New York: Plume, 2008.

9. The study analysed wine reviews in *Wine Spectator*: J. Reuter, 'Does Advertising Bias Product Reviews? An analysis of wine ratings', *Journal of Wine Economics*, 2009, vol. 4, no. 2, pp. 125–51.

10. J. Waldfogel, *Scroogenomics: why you shouldn't buy presents for the holidays*, Princeton, NJ: Princeton University Press, 2009, p. 35. The deadweight calculation is based on summing up Australian Bureau of Statistics retail spending on 'household goods', 'clothing, footwear and personal accessories', 'department store spending' and 'other spending', and estimating the jump in November and December relative to other months of the year. My estimate of $6 billion amounts to gift-buying of about $260 per Australian, a total that is in line with Waldfogel's figure for the United States (US$220 per person in 2007). On occasion, there are reports of much higher figures for 'Christmas spending' (up to $30 billion). These appear to include all spending for the holiday season, rather than trying to specifically identify spending on gifts.

11. M.R. Busse, D.G. Pope, J.C. Pope & J. Silva-Risso, *Projection Bias in the Car and Housing Markets*, National Bureau of Economic Research Working Paper 18212, Cambridge, MA: National Bureau of Economic Research, 2012; U. Simonsohn, 'Weather to go to College', *Economic Journal*, 2010, vol. 120, no. 543, pp. 270–80; D.T. Gilbert, M.J. Gill & T.D. Wilson, 'The Future is Now: Temporal correction in affective forecasting', *Organizational Behavior and Human Decision Processes*, 2002, vol. 88, no. 1, pp. 430–44; D. Ariely, & G. Loewenstein, 'The Heat of the Moment: The effect of sexual arousal on sexual decision making', *Journal of Behavioral Decision Making*, 2006, vol. 19, no. 2, pp. 87–98.

12. S. Iyengar, *The Art of Choosing*, New York: Twelve, 2010, pp. 89–90.

Acknowledgements

I'm a late comer to economics. When I first went to university, I studied government and law. After graduating, I worked as a corporate lawyer, as a High Court associate to Justice Michael Kirby and a political adviser in the UK and Australia. But the more I read on the problems I cared about—from reducing inequality in Australia to promoting growth in the world economy—the more I felt that they couldn't be solved without thinking about incentives, trade-offs, supply and demand and so on.

My decision to study at the Harvard Kennedy School was due in large part to my high school friend Justin Wolfers. Justin and his partner, Betsey Stevenson, apply economic principles to their own lives more than any other couple I know. (Heading off to change the nappy of their new baby, Justin remarked to me with a grin, 'Betsey does inputs, I do outputs.') Since the late 1990s, Justin and I have co-authored a dozen op-eds and a couple of academic papers. Had it not been for my friendship with Justin, I doubt that I would have written this book.

Within a month of starting to study economics at Harvard, I was hooked, and soon switched from a master's to a PhD. Over the next four years, I enjoyed the benefit of marvellous thesis advisers (David Ellwood, Caroline Hoxby, Christopher Jencks), whip-smart classmates (including Raj Chetty, Seema Jayachandran, Ben Olken, Emily Oster and Jonah Rockoff), excellent seminars and a desk for a couple of years at the National Bureau of Economic Research.

After graduating, I was lucky enough to join a group of research-focused economists at the Australian National University. It was delightful to have colleagues such as Alison Booth, Bob Breunig, Bruce Chapman, Deborah Cobb-Clark, Paul Frijters, Bob Gregory, Tim Hatton, Warwick McKibbin, Xin Meng and Chris Ryan, as well as PhD students like Paul Burke, Dinuk Jayasuriya, Daniel Suryadarma and Michelle Tan. I had three main research assistants, Jenny Chesters, Susanne Schmidt and Elena Varganova, and collaborated with many economists, including Alison Booth, Ian Davidoff, Joshua Gans, Christine Neill and Chris Ryan. Visits to the University of Michigan, New York University, Melbourne Business School and the Research Institute of Industrial Economics in Stockholm kept the ideas flowing.

Some of the ideas in this book found their genesis as op-ed columns for Australian newspapers. I thank the editors who published my work, particularly Greg Earl, Joanne Gray, Bill Pheasant and Ben Potter from the *Australian Financial Review*, who provided me with a regular column from 2007 to 2010. I am also grateful to presenter Richard Aedy and producer Amanda Armstrong for a regular 'Wryside Economics' segment on ABC Radio National's *Life Matters* program in 2009 and 2010.

Thank you to Tim Minchin for his permission to quote from his song 'If I didn't have you' and to Edward Mendelson, W.H. Auden's literary executor for allowing me to quote lines from 'As I walked out one evening'.

I'm by no means the first Australian to produce an economics book aimed at a general audience. Previous antipodean popularisers of economics include microeconomists Gigi Foster, Paul Frijters, Joshua Gans, Ross Gittins and Jessica Irvine, and macroeconomists Andrew Charlton, Tim Harcourt and John Quiggin. Conveying research results without dumbing them down can be undervalued both by academics and journalists, and Australia is fortunate to have such a strong team toiling in the interstices of these two occupations.

In writing this book, I am indebted to a multitude of researchers, including Pat Corbett, Peter Deutscher, Alexandra Downie, Matilda Gillis, Eleanor Hewitt, Trishna Malhi, Griffen Murphy, Andrew Palm and Arthur Sun. My friend Sandy Pitcher told me about the '$2 per wear' rule of thumb for clothing purchases. For suggestions on sport, thanks to Bob Gregory, Gus Little, Richard Marles and Lionel Page. Nicholas Rohde generously updated his rankings of best cricket batsmen. Ross Booth and Jeff Borland kindly shared data on AFL club expenditure. I am grateful to the anonymous colleague—described here as 'Matthew'—whose story begins Chapter 4.

Leon Berkelmans shared the archival material from his unpublished work on the performance of the *Age* panel of economic forecasters. Damien Hickman carried out the exercise of seeing how betting favourites perform in a tipping competition, and Thomas McMahon shared the results of pursuing the same strategy in his workplace. Kym Anderson shared both insights and data relating to wine forecasting. Clare Wright provided me with data on gender ratios on the goldfields. Justin Wolfers and Deborah Cobb-Clark particularly shaped my views on the economics of the family.

Speaking of family, my brother Tim Leigh let me use his story in Chapter 9, and my parents, Barbara and Michael Leigh, provided valuable feedback on earlier drafts. Others who gave me comments on previous iterations include Kym Anderson, Alison Booth, Jeff Borland, Bob Breunig, Jim Chalmers, Andrew Charlton, Deborah Cobb-Clark, Michael Cooney, Michael Coutts-Trotter, Macgregor Duncan, Paul Frijters, Michael Fullilove, David Galenson, Joshua Gans, Tanya Greeves, Nicholas Gruen, Colm Harmon, Jessica Irvine, Gweneth Leigh, Richard Marles, Helen Maxwell, Julie McKay, Thomas McMahon, Alex Millmow, Melanie Poole, John Quiggin, Peter Siminski, Anne Summers, Nick Terrell, Tim Watts and Justin Wolfers. Thanks also to my Allen & Unwin team, particularly my publisher Elizabeth Weiss, editors Susan Keogh and Belinda Lee, designer Lisa White and publicist Jane Symmans.

My talented parliamentary staff are a joy to work with, and surprisingly tolerant about having a book-writing boss. As an MP,

I've engaged in conversations about economics with parliamentarians from across the political spectrum. In the Labor caucus, I'm fortunate to work with a group of parliamentarians who recognise the power of markets, but aren't in thrall to them.

Finally, this book is dedicated to my remarkable wife Gweneth and our three energetic boys, Sebastian, Theodore and Zachary. Fam-Leigh: thank you for tolerating my relentless and unflinching use of incentives. In Auden's immortal words from 'As I Walked Out One Evening':

> *I'll love you till the ocean*
> *Is folded and hung up to dry*
> *And the seven stars go squawking*
> *Like geese about the sky.'*

INDEX

inheritance taxes 3
international trade negotiations
148

Karlan, Dean 36-7
stickK website 35-6
Keen, Steve 157, 225
Klein, Richard
Cigarettes are Sublime
34-5
Kloppers, Marius 182-3, 232
Kngwarreye, Emily Kane 97
Knight, Julian 109-11
Knox, Malcolm 52
Kortt, Michael 75-6

labour markets, forecasting
162-4, 227
Lambert, George 94-5
lemmings 11, 190
Levitt, Steven 119, 121, 184
Freakonomics 121
life
expectancy 48, 199
statistical value of 116
lightening fatalities 217
Lima, Jaqueline 133-4, 221
Lindsay, Joan 106, 216
Lindsay, Norman 106 216
'lookism' discrimination 78

Malkiel, Burton 165
Malouf, David 104, 215

margin, decisions at the 5, 187
market equilibrium 14
Marles, Richard 202
marriage contract 22-3
engagement rings 23
gender imbalance 181
mortality rates 189-90
Mount Isa 13-14, 191
movie directors 91

Namatjira, Albert 97
Natural Resource Charter
145-6
Neill, Christine 114
Nelson, Robert 94
Nolan, Sidney 94, 212
novelists 90-1, 101-8
career cycles 103
top Australian 102, 215
'nowcasting' 171-3, 230

Olympics 202
medals and GDP relationship
63-5, 202
online dating 17-18, 191
optimal-stopping problem
16-17

Park, Ruth 104-5, 216
'Peltzman effect' 38, 195
Perry Preschool program 127,
220
Picasso, Pablo 90